SAINTS
AND
FEASTS
OF THE
CATHOLIC CALENDAR

VOLUME TWO OF FOUR
APRIL - JUNE

SAINTS
...............AND...............
FEASTS
............OF THE............
CATHOLIC CALENDAR

VOLUME TWO OF FOUR

APRIL - JUNE

FR. MICHAEL BLACK

Scripture quotations from the New Revised Standard Version Bible: Catholic Edition, copyright © 1989, 1993 National Council of the Churches of Christ in the United States of America. Used by permission. All rights reserved worldwide.

No part of this book not already in the public domain, except for a total of one reflection of one calendar day, may be reproduced or stored, in any form, either in print or digitally, without the prior permission of the publisher. If any copyrighted material has been used in this work without proper credit or attribution being given, please contact the publisher in writing so that future printings may be corrected accordingly.

Cover design by the author and Opus Creative Studio; Interior art by George Angelini, with permission, by Opus Creative Studio, and courtesy of public domain images from the Te Papa Museum, New Zealand, the Getty Museum Open Content Program, and Wiki-Commons. Copyright ©2022. Fr. Michael Black, all rights reserved.

TABLE OF CONTENTS

Notes	viii
Poem: Under a Roman Slab	x
Introduction	1

APRIL — **Page**

2	St. Francis of Paola	4
4	St. Isidore	6
5	St. Vincent Ferrer	8
7	St. John Baptiste de la Salle	10
11	St. Stanislaus	13
13	St. Martin	15
21	St. Anselm	17
23	St. Adalbert	20
23	St. George	22
24	St. Fidelis of Sigmaringen	24
25	St. Mark	27
28	St. Peter Chanel	29
28	St. Louis Grignion de Montfort	31
29	St. Catherine of Siena	34
30	St. Pius V	36

MAY — **Page**

1	St. Joseph the Worker	40
2	St. Athanasius	42
3	SS. Philip and James	45
10	St. Damien de Veuster of Moloka'i	47

10	Saint John of Ávila	49
12	SS. Nereus and Achilleus	51
12	St. Pancras	53
13	Our Lady of Fatima	55
14	St. Matthias	58
15	St. Isidore	60
18	St. John I	63
20	St. Bernadine of Siena	65
21	St. Christopher Magallanes and Companions	67
22	St. Rita of Cascia	71
25	St. Bede the Venerable	73
25	St. Gregory VII	75
25	St. Mary Magdalene de' Pazzi	77
26	St. Phillip Neri	79
27	St. Augustine of Canterbury	81
29	St. Paul VI	84
31	Visitation of the Blessed Virgin Mary	86

JUNE **Page**

1	St. Justin Martyr	90
2	SS. Marcellinus and Peter	92
3	St. Charles Lwanga	94
5	St. Boniface	97
6	St. Norbert	99
9	St. Ephrem	101
11	St. Barnabas	103
13	St. Anthony of Padua	105

19	St. Romuald	107
21	St. Aloysius Gonzaga	110
22	St. Paulinus of Nola	113
22	SS. John Fisher and Thomas More	115
24	Birth of St. John the Baptist	117
26	St. Josemaria Escriva	120
27	St. Cyril of Alexandria	122
28	St. Irenaeus of Lyon	124
29	SS. Peter and Paul	127
30	First Martyrs of the Church of Rome	129
	Poem: The Swirling Soul	131

HOLY WEEK & MOVEABLE FEASTS

Palm Sunday of the Lord's Passion	134
Holy Thursday	136
Good Friday	138
Easter Sunday	142
Divine Mercy Sunday	145
Ascension of the Lord	148
Pentecost Sunday	150
The Blessed Virgin Mary, Mother of the Church	153
The Most Holy Trinity	155
The Most Holy Body and Blood of Christ	158
Sacred Heart of Jesus	160
Immaculate Heart of Mary	162

NOTES ON VOLUME TWO AND THIS SERIES

❖ Many saints and blesseds are the official patrons of more than one place, activity, thing, or class of people. Many saints and blesseds are also, by custom or mere digital rumor, the unofficial patrons of various other places, activities, things, or classes of people. The saintly patronages cited herein are accurate but not exhaustive. Some more obscure saints lack any patronage at all.

❖ Spellings of saint and place names are often according to their original language, but not exclusively so.

❖ The cover of Volume II shows, in clockwise order, simulated passport stamps, with their corresponding feast days, for St. Damian de Veuster, St. Charles Lwanga, St. Anthony of Padua, St. Thomas More, and St. Catherine of Siena. The cover design conveys a sense of the Church's geographical and chronological reach. As the reader briefly immerses herself in the lives of individual saints, she will cross the borders of Europe, Asia, the Americas, and Africa. She will move up and down the centuries, walking the international terrain of the universal Church to briefly meet the friends of God whose deep faith and iron-clad virtue shone so brightly both in times long past and, through the liturgy, even today. It is hoped that the cover implicitly conveys that to be an informed Catholic is to be a wise, well-travelled, two- thousand-year-old person. It is to be not just a citizen of the world as it is, but of the world as it was and always will be.

❖ Although the word "feast" is commonly used indiscriminately to refer to any holy day, the Church uses more precise categories: *Solemnity*, *Feast*, *Memorial*, and *Optional Memorial*. On certain days of Lent and Advent, a *Memorial* has traditionally been referred to as a *Commemoration*. The Church does not, however, officially use the term *Commemoration* apart from All Souls Day. The liturgical designations cited herein are accurate, though not as fully elaborated as in an Ordo. The subtleties by which the Catholic liturgical calendar operates are not detailed.

❖ The dates of birth and of death of some saints are either totally unknown or disputed by different sources. The letter "c" stands for the Latin *circa*, "about," and is employed when the saint's specific dates are unknown. When a date is disputed among reputable sources, the date given in *Butler's Lives* is generally cited, although not always so.

❖ The "Catholic Calendar" of the title refers, more specifically, to the sanctoral calendar of the Roman Missal, Third Typical Edition, 2002 (English Language Edition 2011). Saint and feast days inserted into the universal sanctoral calendar subsequent to 2011 by the Congregation for Divine Worship and Discipline of the Sacraments are incorporated into this series through the end of 2021. The liturgical calendar of the United States Conference of Catholic Bishops, which adds some North American saints to the universal calendar, is normative for this series.

❖ Thousands of men and women have been canonized by the Congregation for the Causes of Saints and its predecessor Congregations. Many saints, however, date from the pre-Congregation era of the first millennium, when popular acclamation, local episcopal approbation, or long custom were sufficient to confer the title "saint." Only a small percentage of all these stars of holiness shine brightly enough to be included on the Church's universal calendar. It is precisely this constellation of "all-star" saints, and only those saints, who are presented in this series, rather than every single saint known to the Church's long history.

UNDER A ROMAN SLAB

Paul, Sixth that name holding,
sage of gray hair, taught,
slowing cold gusts blowing
confusion down the halls.

Father, chain of ages linking,
firm in Peter's chair, wrote,
showing bold truth knowing
Malthus' gross shortfall.

The world, hale body fixing,
conscience unaware, heard,
complaining its lusts reining
from a gallop to a crawl.

Couples, dazed ideas clearing,
far from all mad air, read,
spacing love's embracing
new life with proper awe.

Neighbors, married life unwinding,
little love to cheer, mused,
reflecting that rejecting
life made Eden fall.

The celibate, family name erasing,
leaving not an heir, thought,
seeding fields now teeming
with life's harvest and windfall.

The priest, content alone toiling,
year surpassing year, sowed,
broadcasting truths everlasting
for reward when trumpets call.

Children, of true love offspringing,
born of nature's pair, live,
unknowing the hard going
that sparked their life at all.

Pilgrims, to St. Peter's trekking,
absorbed in grateful prayer, kneel,
avowing heads now bowing
to the wisdom of Pope Paul.

Paul, under a Roman slab,
tomb stark and spare, rests,
interceding those souls' pleading
mercy like stunned Saul.

A sinner, humble heart melting,
new life soon to bear, whispers,
repenting of dissenting
from truth and natural law.

A voice, small not overwhelming,
afloat in solemn air, replies,
correcting time neglecting
his brave stance: "I'm canonized!"

M.B.

Pope St. Paul VI was the Bishop of Rome from 1963-1978. He was canonized by Pope Francis on October 14, 2018. He is buried among the papal tombs under St. Peter's Basilica. His feast day is May 29.

INTRODUCTION

The creed recited in the African Church of early Christianity was similar to the Roman creed except that in addition to enumerating the Church's marks as one, holy, catholic, and apostolic, the African faithful also professed *"Credo in…sanctam matrem ecclesiam."* "I believe in holy *mother* Church." How evocative!

Our Church is not a mother merely by analogy. Catholicism is not a collection of individuals who each discovered Jesus in his own way and in his own time and then just happened to come together to share that common belief in the same place. The Church gathers, she is not gathered. She is a mother, not a sister to her equal. Mother Church is not the fruit of the gathering she herself generated any more than parents emanate from their children. The Church is born not from her faithful but from the side of the crucified Christ. Her origin is theological, not sociological. If there were only one Catholic, the Church would still exist in her fullness. The same Church born from Christ's side was baptized with the scorching breath of the Holy Spirit breathed on her at Pentecost, fortifying her with the divine gifts she imparts to the faithful through the Sacraments.

Holy Mother Church has generated some select sons and daughters of heroic virtue who are publicly recognized for their holiness. *Volume II* of *Saints and Feasts of the Catholic Calendar* relates more piercing stories of the generous men and women who have done their sacramental Mother due honor through their lives of high virtue, ardent prayer, and sheer daring for Christ.

A mother protects, a mother nourishes, a mother inspires. Our Mother Church offers us, through her saints, examples enough to protect, nourish, and inspire her faithful living in the world today. To read the stories of the saints is to know our mother more deeply. To emulate those same saints is to make our Lord smile, to gratify our Blessed Mother, and to revivify a Church hungry for our witness.

APRIL

Rich in Mercy

APRIL

April 2: Saint Francis of Paola, Hermit
1416–1507
Optional Memorial; Liturgical Color: White
Patron Saint of Calabria, mariners, and naval officers

He lived a perpetual Lent

The first followers of Saint Francis of Assisi were known as the "Mendicants from Assisi." Yet as the group attracted men and women from all over Italy and beyond, a new name, not specific to Assisi, was needed. Saint Francis named his brotherhood the Ordo Fratrum Minorum (O.F.M.). This is typically translated from the Latin as the Order of Friars Minor, implying that there is an Order of Friars Major. A better translation might be the Order of Lesser Brothers. Saint Francis wanted himself, and all of his brothers, to be less in everything—less prideful, less well known, less wealthy, and less well nourished than anyone else.

Today's saint, the Padre Pio of his era, was a holy priest from the town of Paola in Southern Italy. He was baptized as Francis by his parents when, after several years of going childless, they made a vow to name any son that might be born to them in the great saint's honor. Francis of Paola was worthy of his namesake from a young age. His parents took special care with his religious upbringing and brought him to live for a year in a Franciscan monastery when Francis was just twelve. The young Francis developed a reputation for holiness even when just a teen. By the age of twenty, he was living as a hermit in a cave near Paola when local men began to gather around him. The fledgling group adopted the name "the Hermits of Brother Francis of Assisi," a name later changed to the "Friars Minims," or just "Minims," meaning "less" or "least," in the spirit of the "Lesser Brothers" that Saint Francis of Assisi had founded centuries before.

Francis of Paola desired humility, nothingness, and total self-abnegation. He and his followers lived a perpetual Lent. All Minims took the usual vows of poverty, chastity, and obedience. But they also took a special fourth vow to abstain, all year long and all life long, from meat, eggs, butter, cheese, milk, and all dairy products. The fast never ended. This was mortification on a heroic scale. Vegetarianism, much less veganism, was a step beyond what Saint

APRIL

Francis of Assisi himself had lived. Saint Francis of Assisi ate what was set before him, including meat. He even criticized vegetarian brothers who refused meat, saying such an attitude questioned God's providence and presumed the future, when a brother should instead gratefully accept whatever dish was placed on the table before him.

Francis of Paola's veganism was united to a strict moral code, a community life built around the Sacraments, and a deep spirituality centered on Jesus Christ. To be "one with nature" does not mean to be morally ambiguous or to break with religious traditions. A diet should not be a creed. Saint Francis was organic in that he lived one with God, with nature, with his religious brothers, and with the Church. Francis was perennially concerned with the moral laxity of the Church of his era, and purposefully fasted and did penance in reparation for its sins. While Francis of Assisi lived austerely and suffered debilitating illnesses, he was nevertheless cheerful and animated in his dealings with others. No one ever accused Francis of Paola of being ebullient. He was a fully armed spiritual warrior of the most serious kind. He went barefoot. He slept on a board. He was a desert father without the sand.

After a very long life of fasting, prayer, miracle working, and wide fame for his holiness even outside of Italy, Saint Francis of Paola died in France. His order had by then spread throughout Europe. His reputation for sanctity was such that he was canonized in 1519, only twelve years after his death. In 1562 Protestant Calvinists in France unsealed his tomb and found his body incorrupt. They then desecrated the saint, scattering his remains. Saint Francis of Paola, after sacrificing everything in life, was not allowed to rest in peace. He was strewn about like trash, ensuring that only trace relics of him remained. Saint Francis wanted to be treated as the least of all. His desire was fulfilled both in life and in death.

Saint Francis of Paola, you lived an integrated life deeply united to God, nature, and your fellow man. Intercede before the Trinity in heaven on our behalf, assisting us to grow closer to God through death to self, through prayer, and through a deep attachment to Christ.

APRIL

April 4: Saint Isidore, Bishop and Doctor
c. 560–636
Optional Memorial; Liturgical Color: White
Patron Saint of the internet

There was little he did not know

The vast colonial ambitions of Spain in the sixteenth and seventeenth centuries went hand in hand with equally epic Catholic missionary efforts. This unity of purpose, these shared goals, with civil and ecclesiastical resources and powers working in concert, was the natural consequence of a country with a total unity of identity. Today's saint was a singularly important, if remote, source for that powerful concurrence of Iberian theology, culture, art, and language which, after centuries of gestation, became the Spanish juggernaut that conquered and evangelized a hemisphere in the 1500s.

As a youth, Isidore received an excellent classical education in the Roman tradition, similar to the classical learning Saint Augustine imbibed two centuries before him and utilized to such great effect. Yet Isidore not only learned a great deal, he also remembered it and was uncommonly dedicated to his intellectual pursuits, writing numerous weighty tomes. The breadth and depth of his learning were without equal in his time. It was simply said that Isidore, Archbishop of Seville, knew everything. He is considered by many to be the last of the Latin Fathers of the Church, those early Christian theologians whose writings are the gold standard for all subsequent theologians.

His knowledge was put to good use. As the Roman world, which had dominated Spain for so many centuries, slowly crumbled away in the fifth and sixth centuries, Visigothic (Western Goths) tribes overran Spain. Like their Gothic cousins in Central Europe, the Visigoths were Arians, and Arians were heretics. They denied that Christ was consubstantial with the Father and accepted all that flowed from that erroneous starting point. Saint Isidore played an important role in the assimilation of the Visigoths to Nicene Catholicism after one of their Kings abandoned Arianism. Theological unity having been achieved, the old Roman culture of Iberia slowly blended with Visigothic culture to form something new—Spain. Saint Isidore was, then, a nation builder, because he

APRIL

was first a Church builder. And he built the Church not just through his massive erudition but also through effective headship in calling and guiding Church synods, by establishing liturgical unity through the Mozarabic Rite, and by encouraging scholarship and learning through the Cathedral schools he mandated in every diocese.

Saint Isidore's most enduring work is his *Etymologies* (or *Origins*), an enormous compendium of universal knowledge. It was the standard encyclopedia in Medieval libraries and continued to be utilized as late as the Renaissance. No author's manuscripts were more widely copied in the Middle Ages than Isidore's. Although Saint Isidore was not a creative thinker in the same class as Saint Augustine or the Eastern Fathers of the Church, his mind was such a vast storehouse of knowledge that Pope Saint John Paul II named him the Patron Saint of the Internet.

After a long reign as Archbishop of Seville, in his last days Saint Isidore prepared for death by wearing sackcloth and ashes, confessing his faults to his people in church, and asking their forgiveness. He died in his late seventies in 636, just four years after Mohammed, the founder of Islam, died in Saudi Arabia. About seventy-five years after their deaths, Muslim armies crossed the strait of Gibraltar from North Africa and began the long conquest which obliterated the Visigoths. The Spanish reconquest of their nation would take centuries until, in 1492, the last Muslim stronghold, Granada, fell. Both sides were inspired by faith more than patriotism. Both sides fought. Both sides thought they were right. In the end, the nation Isidore created was the stronger and drove Mohammed's heirs back over the waters to Africa. Isidore's enormous legacy was a Catholic nation, and it prevailed.

Saint Isidore, you used your education and knowledge to great effect to evangelize a people. Help all who seek your intercession to unite their learning with zeal for the good of the Church and the many peoples it serves.

APRIL

April 5: Saint Vincent Ferrer, Priest
c. 1350–1419
Optional Memorial; Liturgical Color: White
Patron Saint of builders

He slept on the floor, fasted endlessly, performed miracles, and converted thousands

Saint Dominic de Guzman, a Spanish priest, founded the Order of Preachers in the early thirteenth century. He wanted to establish an Order of priests who were well educated in theology, adept at preaching the truths they lived, and who had more flexibility than a monastery-bound priest to travel and evangelize. Over a century later, today's saint was born in Saint Dominic's own country, joined the Dominican Order, and carried out in the most dynamic and complete way the essential vision of Saint Dominic. Saint Vincent Ferrer was well educated and a powerfully effective preacher. He travelled almost without cease throughout Western Europe, impacting the lives of untold thousands of people through his example of holiness, his supernatural gifts, and his preaching. Saint Vincent was the ideal Dominican.

Vincent was born in Valencia, on the southern coast of Spain, to an English father and a Spanish mother. He was named in honor of Saint Vincent Martyr, who met his death in the same city in the fourth century. Vincent received an excellent education and earned a doctorate in theology at a young age. It was said that he read exclusively Scripture for three full years and had committed much of it to memory. He taught philosophy and then took up advanced studies, in Barcelona, of Islam and Judaism. Spain had a sizeable minority of Jews, and Muslims still controlled large portions of Southern Spain in Saint Vincent's day. So these studies were not merely theoretical. Saint Vincent converted a large number of Spanish Jews and interacted with Spanish Muslims on a regular basis.

The ecclesial event which most marked our saint's life was the Western Schism of 1378–1418. This painful episode saw two, and eventually three, cardinals claim to be the validly elected pope. This open wound pained the Church for two generations. Some Europeans lived their whole lives knowing only a bitterly divided papacy. The Western Schism proved so intractable a problem, and caused such scandal, that it can be argued that it was the remote spark of the Reformation which caught fire through Northern Europe about one hundred years later. Such were the complexities of the Schism that Saint Vincent found himself on opposite sides of the issue from Saint Catherine of Siena and various other deeply committed Catholics.

St. Vincent Ferrer
Andrea Procaccini

Our saint spent the better part of his life as a tireless itinerant preacher traveling along the highways and the byways of Spain, France, and Italy, drawing enormous crowds, inviting and inspiring them to a deeper life in Christ. Near the end of his life, Vincent's effective preaching played a decisive role at the Council of Constance in 1414. He convinced the Spanish King to cease supporting the very pope who Vincent had previously backed in the Schism. Vincent was man enough to see that his candidate had become an obstacle to Church unity. Vincent thus lived a hard lesson in humility when his man was abandoned, excommunicated, and judged by history to have been an antipope. Saint Vincent fittingly died on one of his incessant missionary journeys, far from home in Northern France, at the age of sixty-nine. His reputation for holiness was such that he was canonized a saint in 1455, within the lifetime of many who had heard him preach.

Saint Vincent Ferrer, you lived a life of fervor and dedication to the truths of the Catholic faith, imparting the education you received to others through your witness and preaching. Come to the aid of all teachers and preachers to emulate your virtues with your same zeal for the house of the Lord.

April 7: Saint John Baptiste de la Salle, Priest
1651–1719
Memorial; Liturgical Color: White
Patron Saint of Christian teachers

Great faith, charm, and skill opened school doors to millions

A cowboy mounts a horse and lassos a calf to show the next cowboy how to wrangle. A fisherman tosses a net into the ocean so that his son learns to put food on the table for dinner. And a good teacher teaches an apprentice how to teach. The passing on of professional knowledge doesn't happen by accident. Those who are skilled teach those who are less so. Today's saint, John Baptiste de la Salle, was a lifelong educator, an excellent teacher who had innovative and effective ideas on how to educate youth. Most importantly, he also had faith, perseverance, and the administrative skills to bring his educational vision to fulfillment in the face of stiff resistance.

A good teacher must do much more than master content. He must do much more than manage his classroom. A good teacher is an artist who combines mastery of the material with psychological insights, discipline, charm, preparedness, and love, all in careful equilibrium. At the time Saint Jean Baptiste began to teach teachers, the custom in France was to teach children Latin. And once they had learned Latin sufficiently, the custom was to teach the students every other subject in Latin. Lower class, poorer children, were often not taught at all or only for a few brief years. Jean Baptiste wanted all children to have access to a good education, for their schooling to be free of charge, and for classes to be in French. These ideals, combined with his own charm, holiness, and refined *savoir faire*, drew many idealistic young men to his side. They wanted to be teachers too, and to dedicate themselves to the Lord. Originally,

APRIL

ST. JOHN BAPTISTE DE LA SALLE
April 7

"Take even more care of the education of the young people entrusted to you than if they were the children of a king."

Jean Baptiste was reluctant to live with, and train, men who belonged to a social class far below his own. He remarked that his first teacher trainees ranked below his own servants. In the end, though, Jean overcame his reluctance and innate prejudice and threw himself wholeheartedly into the educational work that would make him famous.

So many young men gathered around him that Jean Baptiste founded an Order which was, after his death, officially recognized by the Church—the Christian Brothers. Just when his educational apostolates needed funds to expand, Jean Baptiste inherited a fortune from his parents. He was tempted to use the money to open new schools but instead donated it to the poor, deciding to rely only upon providence for the support of his schools. The members of his Order were intentionally not ordained to the Priesthood so that sacramental responsibilities would not distract them from teaching. His Christian Brothers also had no obligation to pray the Divine Office (the Breviary) and were prohibited from physical mortifications beyond the Church's norms on fasting. Jean felt that teaching well was itself a mortification which required heroic self discipline. Jean wanted nothing less than ambassadors of Christ to the young, not just teachers. All of this was novel for its time—a body of men with no ordained members dedicated exclusively to education was unheard of.

For all his successes in opening new schools, however, Jean Baptiste had numerous setbacks. Over many years he was verbally attacked, sued in court, and vilified by some religious Orders and clerics. They saw his free schools and universal educational goals as a threat to their own local monopolies on education. Jean Baptiste dealt with all of this with admirable courage, humility, and magnanimity. It's not easy times that make one great. It's hardship, adversity, and persecution. Jean Baptiste's trials made a good man into a great man, and a great man into a saint. He fasted continually, mortified himself harshly, and traded his early life of comfort for hard scrabble poverty. After relinquishing the heavy burden of his Order's leadership and administration, Jean was so obedient to his successor that the new superior joked that Jean would not die unless he was given permission to do so. The Counter-Reformation fervor behind so many great saints of sixteenth-century Italy and Spain arrived late to France, but it arrived no less ardent. Jean Baptiste was one of its greatest exemplars. The Christians Brothers peaked at over sixteen thousand members in the 1950s and are still active today in numerous countries, operating over a thousand educational institutions. The legacy of their dynamic, innovative, and indefatigable founder continues to thrive.

Saint John Baptiste de la Salle, through your intercession, give all teachers of the Faith the perseverance, grace, and love they need to teach the uneducated, especially the poor and those who struggle to learn. Your determination inspires. Your heavenly assistance guarantees fruitfulness.

April 11: Saint Stanislaus, Bishop and Martyr
1030–1079
Memorial; Liturgical Color: Red
Patron Saint of Poland

Royal fury fells a bishop

For many centuries, the coronation ritual of a king was considered to be a Sacrament of the Church. Such was the importance of the king's role in protecting and promoting the faith in his realm that his enthronement was embellished with a liturgical pomp and splendor similar to the ordination rite of a bishop. The sacramental character of a king's coronation was not reflected, however, in the ritual by which a woman became a queen. Only a man could be crowned, in the same way that only a man could receive Holy Orders. The parallel duties which kings and bishops owed to both Church and Kingdom sometimes led to irresolvable conflicts. Bishops resented kings infringing upon ecclesiastical affairs, while kings resented bishops meddling in civil matters. Since civil and religious life was, until very modern times, utterly intermingled in most cultures, the high tensions generated by the nearly co-equal powers and responsibilities of kings and bishops inevitably led to bloodshed.

The blood of today's saint was spilled precisely due to such high tension. Saint Stanislaus was the Bishop of Krakow, Poland, in the century just after that nation's baptism after the conversion of its king. Saint Stanislaus had various and serious disputes with Poland's

APRIL

King Bolesław II: over property, over a war, and over the King's moral failings. This led to Stanislaus excommunicating Bolesław, in seeming support of the King's enemies. Although the precise details of this King-Bishop conflict have been lost to history, it is clear that Bolesław was outraged by Stanislaus' sanction and labelled him a traitor. When the King entered Krakow's Cathedral for Mass, the service was immediately halted due to his excommunication. Bolesław went into a fury and actively sought Stanislaus' blood. The henchmen the King sent to assassinate Bishop Stanislaus, however, refused to carry out the deed. So King Bolesław entered through the doors of the chapel outside the city where the Bishop was saying Mass and cut Stanislaus down himself. Bishop Stanislaus was immediately venerated as a martyr, his relics were transferred to the Cathedral, and he was canonized a saint a century and a half after his death. For centuries, Polish kings were crowned at the splendid tomb of the martyr in the central nave of Krakow's Cathedral. Saint Stanislaus is one of the patron saints of Poland, being especially venerated in the Archdiocese of Krakow.

On November 1, 1946, a young Polish man named Karol Wojtyła, in love with God and country, was ordained a priest and celebrated his first Masses in Krakow's Cathedral of Saint Stanislaus. Father Wojtyła went on to become the seventy-sixth Archbishop of Krakow. He later became a Cardinal and then Pope John Paul II. He is now a saint. Pope Saint John Paul II had a great devotion to Saint Stanislaus and often prayed at his tomb. The Pope even planned his first pastoral visit to Poland to coincide exactly with the nine-hundredth anniversary of the saint's martyrdom. John Paul II's trip missed the exact anniversary, due to a lack of cooperation from the communist government, but the pope didn't miss the year. 1979 turned out to be a pivotal year for Poland. The papal pilgrimage unleashed social movements that brought communism to its knees a decade later. The memory of long-ago Saint Stanislaus, then, played a remote role in conquering an unjust modern government.

Many details about the life of Saint Stanislaus are lost in the fog of the past. Only a basic outline of his life is possible. But his heroic example, precisely as a bishop, gave Karol Wojtyła a model to follow in his own life as a Polish bishop and Pope in far different circumstances of civil and ecclesiastical tension than those of the eleventh century. We can speculate that on May 13, 1981, when Pope John Paul II was shot and almost killed by a state-sponsored assassin, he thought of the state-sponsored attack which ended Saint Stanislaus' life so many centuries before. Civil and Church power still clash, even in modern times, as the 1980 murder of the El Salvadoran Archbishop Saint Oscar Romero also proves. Pope John Paul II survived, thank God, perhaps through the intercession of the great patron of Poland we celebrate today.

Saint Stanislaus, you fearlessly confronted those who threatened the well-being of the Church, and so gave a heroic example of martyrdom to an entire nation. Help all who seek your intercession to be as brave and forthright as you in the face of threats and adversity.

April 13: Saint Martin I, Pope and Martyr
c. 590–655
Memorial; Liturgical Color: Red

Exiled, abandoned, starving, a Pope dies for sound theology

After being elected the Bishop of Rome in 649, today's saint called a local Council which established the correct theology of the Church regarding the two wills of Christ. For this teaching and its broad dissemination, Martin was abducted in Rome by emissaries of the Byzantine Emperor Constans II, brought to Constantinople, and humiliated. Martin refused to retract or bend to the Emperor's incorrect theology, which denied that Christ had a human will. Martin was imprisoned, publicly flogged, maltreated, condemned for treason, and exiled from Constantinople to the Crimean Peninsula on the Black Sea. And there the Pope died—naked, starving, forgotten, and alone—far from Rome, in the year 655, a victim of bad theology and the last pope, so far, venerated as a martyr.

The Council of Chalcedon in 451 had synthesized centuries of theological debate by teaching, authoritatively, that the divine nature of the Second Person of the Trinity and the human nature of Jesus were distinct but united in the one person of Jesus Christ. This merging of natures in one person is called the hypostatic union. The Son of God, then, truly took flesh and experienced all things, save sin, that a man experiences. So when Jesus said, "I am thirsty" (Jn

19:28), He didn't mean to say, "Just my human nature is thirsty." And when His majestic voice echoed off the stone walls of Bethany calling, "Lazarus, come out!" (Jn 11:43), He didn't mean to say, "The divine nature inside of me, and only the divine nature, says 'Lazarus, Come Out!'"

Yet Eastern Christians, primarily in Egypt and Syria, clung to a Monophysite, or one nature, theology of Jesus Christ long after Chalcedon had settled the matter. The Second Council of Constantinople in 553 attempted, unsuccessfully, to pull the Monophysites back into the orbit of Chalcedon. By the 600s, tensions between Chalcedonians and Monophysites were a political problem for the Byzantine empire. So some Eastern theologians, supported by the Emperor, looked for common ground and proposed a one-willed Christ, instead of a one-natured Christ. This one-will heresy is called Monothelitism (monos = one; thelos = will). The issue of Christ's will(s) had never been formally resolved, so the Emperor hoped a one-willed, instead of a one-natured, Christ would placate the Monophysites and unite his theologically diverse subjects.

Chalcedon's teaching on Christ's two natures was ontological, or just logical, and did not explain how a person operates with dual intellects and wills. Monothelitists argued that if Christ's two natures could seamlessly unite in one person, then so could His two wills. There was no human will in Christ, the argument went, because it was totally subsumed into the mightier divine will. But Pope Martin and others knew that this was theologically impossible, since a Christ without a functioning human will would have been a zombie, a ghost of a man. Nor could one argue that Jesus had one will divided into a divine and a human sphere, as Jesus was not a schizophrenic with a split identity.

Martin's theology of the two wills was vindicated after his death when it was explicitly defined by the Third Council of Constantinople in 681. This Council taught Christ's human will was "in subjection to his divine and all-powerful will." That is, Christ's two wills were separate in their natures but freely united in their object. How do two wills inside of one person enter into communion? In the same way that two wills in two different persons enter into communion. Each will gives free and independent assent to a principle, idea, or truth shared with the other will. The two wills retain their independence but freely unite in their assent to a common value. Thus Jesus' human will, in total freedom, submitted to the will of the Son of God.

During his captivity, Martin was hurt by the indifference which the Church of Saint Peter in Rome paid to one of their own. Martin was also deeply pained when a new Pope was elected though he was still alive. It is every pope's duty to preserve the unity and integrity of the Church by preserving the unity and integrity of Christ. Martin did just that. The fruits of Martin's martyrdom advanced theology toward its correct conclusion on Christ's two wills in the decades after he died, even though poor Martin himself has been largely forgotten. His remains were returned to the Eternal City after his death and he now rests in peace somewhere under the marble floor of Saint Peter's Basilica.

Pope Saint Martin I, through your intercession before the Father in Heaven, fortify all teachers and leaders of the Church to remain steadfast in the truth, to advocate for the truth, and to suffer for the truth, no matter the personal cost.

April 21: Saint Anselm, Bishop and Doctor
c. 1033–1109
Optional Memorial; Liturgical Color: White

His pen pierced the blue sheet above, revealing God

Few bishops have been canonized as saints since the Catholic Counter-Reformation of the sixteenth and seventeenth centuries. The earlier history of the Church is, however, replete with saintly bishops. In the patristic era, in the first few centuries after Christ, a vast constellation of saintly bishops shined on the Church. Today's saint was a scholar bishop in the mold of the educated churchmen of an earlier time. Saint Anselm was a world-class thinker, a politically aware defender of the Church's rights, a contemplative monk, a faithful son of the pope, and the greatest philosopher of the eleventh century.

Saint Anselm entered the Monastery of Bec in Normandy, France, as a young man and quickly impressed his superiors with his character and incisive mind. He was elected prior, then abbot, at a young age. He was a deeply prayerful abbot who was close to his monks and who hated to be away from the cloister. The monastery had many dealings with England due to its close proximity to that country, though, so Anselm travelled there regularly. These visits eventually led to his appointment as the Archbishop of Canterbury. Anselm spent many years as archbishop in conflict with English civil power over who had the authority to "invest," or empower, a bishop with the symbols of office at his installation Mass. The lay investiture controversy was a long simmering dispute throughout Europe. It was eventually resolved in favor of the Church's right to invest its bishops with crozier, miter, and ring.

Much more than his role as a pastor in church-state conflicts, Saint Anselm's most enduring legacy is as a philosopher and theologian. Thinking was his avocation even as the monastery was his vocation. Anselm's famous definition of theology as "Faith seeking understanding" has guided centuries of Christian thinkers. Anselm was a working intellectual who produced erudite works on a range of complex subjects. He is the originator, in particular, of the ontological argument for the existence of God. The argument is ontological (or just "logical") in that it is not empirical (scientifically verifiable). It does not argue from outward in, starting with external, observable evidence and then moving toward internal conclusions. The argument is powered, instead, by the raw strength of reason itself. As an example of a reason-driven argument, no one needs to search the world over for square circles to conclude that square circles don't exist. Circles are round, by definition. And no one needs to interview every single bachelor to know that a bachelor is male. A bachelor is, by definition, male. Similarly, the very definition of God, Anselm's holds, is proof that God exists.

Anselm argued that God is a being than which none greater can be imagined. Supposing that the mind can imagine nothing greater than God, and further supposing that what exists in reality is greater than what exists only in the mind, then God must exist in reality. God's non-existence is, then, logically impossible. This argument assumes that the maximum, or upper limit, to what the mind can attribute to God is self-contained in the meaning of the word God. No such upper limit exists in defining pain, temperature, length, or numbers,

APRIL

ST. ANSELM
April 21

"Come now, insignificant man, fly for a moment from your affairs, escape for a little while from the tumult of your thoughts. Put aside now your weighty cares and leave your wearisome toils. Abandon yourself for a little to God and rest for a little in Him."

for example. A longer line can always be drawn, a greater number imagined, a sharper pain experienced, or a hotter temperature described. But to imagine a being greater than God would just be to imagine God more fully. As long as the mind's concept of God is rational, then the argument is convincing. Anselm's nuanced argument has provoked centuries of sophisticated commentary.

Anselm's life began among the Alps of today's Northern Italy, a land of jagged, snow-encrusted mountains which stand over the green valleys below. One night the boy Anselm, asleep in his remote valley home, had a vision. He was called to the court of God on a high summit. Ascending to the very peak of a mountain, he entered the presence of the royal court and sat at the feet of the Master. God asked the boy who he was and where he came from. Anselm answered well and was rewarded with sweet bread from heaven. And then he woke up. Anselm never forgot this dream. He recounted it, in detail, many decades later, to the fellow monk who wrote his first biography. Saint Anselm's mind never really came down from that high court he first visited in a childhood dream. He walked in the highest ranges, above the clouds, hiking from summit to summit, his pen piercing the blue sky to gaze directly into the realm above.

We ask your intercession, Saint Anselm, to help our faith to understand its object. You did not leave man's sense of wonder unchallenged but sought to organize human thought to meet the challenge of God. Help all thinkers to be open to finding as much as searching.

April 23: Saint Adalbert, Bishop and Martyr
956–997
Optional Memorial; Liturgical Color: Red
Patron Saint of the Czech Republic and Poland

Pagans cut down a courageous bishop in the frozen North

Old, stodgy, traditional Catholic Europe in tension with new, liberal, flexible Europe is not a new dichotomy. A millennium ago the roles were reversed. It was old, stodgy, traditional pagan Europe in tension with new, groundbreaking, and progressive Catholic Europe. As the missionary monks, abbots, and bishops of Europe fanned out, ever northward and ever eastward, into upper Germany,

APRIL

Scandinavia, Poland, and the Baltics, they met the warrior tribes and painted chieftains of old Europe, men with skin like bark. These forest clans gathered in sacred groves to offer sacrifice to their pagan idols under the broad canopies of large oaks. In these open-air temples, they butchered prisoners of war and cattle in offerings to their dark powers, sprinkling the blood of the slain on their bodies. Yet from the eighth through the eleventh centuries, missionaries poured into these remote lands, shining the light of the Gospel into its darkest corners. Teutonic and Norse paganism, for all of its unwritten creeds of courage and manliness, was doomed. It was strong, but the Church was stronger. Paganism could not stop vital, solid, well-organized Catholicism with its coherent monotheism, sacred worship, Ten Commandments, self-sacrificing missionaries, and its Gospel of love and respect for all.

The Catholic Church does not arrive to a mission territory, however, as a full-fledged institution. The Church arrives in a person who embodies all that the Church teaches and symbolizes. This person *is* the Church to those he encounters. Today's saint was one of the first missionary bishops to penetrate into the lands of Prussia, in Northeastern Germany. And for daring to preach the Gospel to coarse men, he was murdered on the frigid coast of the Baltic Sea. The Prussians thought he was a Polish spy, and a pagan priest upset at the disruptions Adalbert was causing in Prussian society commanded his death. Saint Adalbert's lifeless body was ransomed for its weight in gold by a Polish king and returned to Poland. He was eventually canonized as Saint Adalbert of Prague, since he was born and raised in Bohemia. He remains a saint equally claimed by both the Polish and Czech people and a seminal figure in early medieval Europe.

Courageous men like Saint Adalbert don't just happen. They are forged over time in red hot fires. Adalbert had a long, difficult, and interesting ecclesiastical career before giving his life for the faith. He was baptized as Vojtěch. But he was so impressed with the saintly German Bishop named Adalbert who taught him, that he took his tutor's name at Confirmation. Adalbert was then named Bishop of Prague at a young age, a consecration whose responsibilities turned him into a far more serious Christian. He quickly matured into his exalted vocation. Bishop Adalbert started aggressively challenging the people of his diocese to shed their pre-Christian customs and to learn what it meant to be true children of God. But Adalbert had a strong temperament and came from a noble family with serious enemies, all of which led him to abandon his diocese twice and flee to Rome. In the Eternal City, he came to know the Benedictines and lived as a monk for several months. Later he would establish Benedictine monasteries in the North in the hope of holding the Christian ground he gained. And to the North he always returned: to Bohemia, to Germany, to Hungary, and to Poland. He was a multilingual and multicultural Pan Slavic Bishop fully equipped to evangelize throughout Central and Eastern Europe.

The rough Prussian people who murdered Adalbert were not fully conquered and converted until 1239, when the Teutonic Knights planted themselves in that land more than two hundred years after Saint Adalbert's death. Yet somebody had to take the first step on the long journey of converting the Prussians. Someone first had to hear "No" a thousand times before someone unknown, much later, ever heard "Yes." Adalbert heard "No" first and died for it. His body absorbed the blows so that other bodies could walk safely. His suffering and death proved that he, an educated man, was just as sturdy as the rugged men he sought to convert, and so was worthy of adding the title of martyr to that of bishop and monk.

Saint Adalbert, we ask that you intercede before God to make all missionaries as courageous as you were, willing to place themselves in difficult situations for the good of the Church. By your example, may we be brave witnesses to the fact that death is sometimes preferable to life.

April 23: Saint George, Martyr
c. Late Third Century
Optional Memorial; Liturgical Color: Red
<u>Patron Saint of England, the nation of Georgia, and scouting</u>

Widely venerated, historically elusive, his legacy is massive

Saint George suffered martyrdom in Palestine before the reign of Constantine. And that is all that can be said with certainty about Saint George. Yet where the documentary record is lacking, other traditions suffice. No one, after all, can document why we blow out candles on a birthday cake, where this nearly universal custom

APRIL

originated, or in what century it even began. Someone, somewhere, for some reason, thought it was a lovely thing to do, and started doing it, otherwise it would not be done today. But questions of where, when, and why fade when friends and family gather around their loved one in the dark, the simple joy on their faces captured in the flickering of the candlelight. Knowing the origin of a tradition matters, since it may reveal unappreciated depths to a common practice. But that a healthy tradition continues is more significant than knowing, or explaining, where it came from. Few Christians can explain the hypostatic union, but everyone loves to unwrap a gift on Christmas morning. No one can determine where and when Saint Valentine lived and died, but our lips broaden into a smile when we open a card on Saint Valentine's Day. A good tradition conveys meaning implicitly whether its origin is obscure or not.

If traditions age like wine, then the traditions surrounding Saint George are of the rarest vintage. Devotion to Saint George is so ancient, so deeply rooted, and so cross cultural that to argue that it rose like a chimera from the hot desert sands would be ridiculous. In the remote valleys of the Judean Desert east of Jerusalem, clinging to the copper-colored cliffs shooting straight up from a wadi, is an ancient monastery named Saint George. It was founded in the fifth century. And amid the stately Roman ruins of Jerash, in Jordan, are the remaining stone walls and mosaic floors of the Church of Saint George, built around 530 A.D. Official devotion to Saint George manifests itself, then, in some of the oldest Christian structures in the Holy Land.

The murky origins of these early buildings merged with written traditions from centuries after George's death until, over time, Saint George was known as a chivalrous knight who died for his faith under the Emperor Diocletian. The lore of a mounted warrior for Christ was immensely appealing to the Crusaders who populated the Holy Land in the twelfth and thirteenth centuries. They transported the hagiography of Saint George back to Europe with them. Oral tradition and popular custom then did its slow work until the ancient Palestinian devotion to Saint George was revived in a new age for new people in new lands. From the Byzantine East to the Latin West, from the Mediterranean South to the Saxon North, few saints became as popular as Saint George. He was named the patron of an enormous number of castles, kingdoms, churches, abbeys, cities, and orders, and even of England itself, where his dragon-slaying exploits still resonate in that country's national mythology.

Traditions hold that Saint George was among the many soldier-martyrs of early Christianity who, instead of dying to protect the Emperor, were killed on the Emperor's orders for refusing to deny Christ. A loyal soldier obeys his master and is prepared to offer his life for a higher good. Roman soldiers were naturally prepared to die for the faith, and many did, killed by their fellows perhaps with some regret. Though the legends swirling around Saint George cannot be verified, they have been accepted by the faithful of many nations for many centuries. Acceptance of traditions is a cultural sieve straining chunks of absurdity from the liquid truth. Saint George has passed through that filter all the stronger. He died for the faith when many of his contemporaries did not—and only the greatest of men did that.

Saint George, you were a loyal soldier and humble Christian who gave your life for Christ. Inspire us to have your same loyalty, your same courage, and your same nobility to die for a mighty cause, whether all at once or bit by bit over time.

April 24: Saint Fidelis of Sigmaringen, Priest and Martyr
1577–1622
Optional Memorial; Liturgical Color: Red
Patron Saint of lawyers & the Congregation for the Evangelization of Peoples

His murderers cut a leg off his dead body in retaliation for his many journeys

To understand the historical and religious context for today's saint, consider an event that took place fifty years before he was born. On January 5, 1527, in Zurich, Switzerland, a young man named Felix Mantz was taken hold of by local officials, had his hands and feet bound to a pole, and was rowed out in a boat to the deepest part of the local river. With a large crowd watching from the shores, he was tossed overboard into the dark water and immediately drowned to death. Felix Mantz's crime? He believed only adults should be baptized, not children. Mantz was not killed by the Inquisition, the

APRIL

St. Fidelis of Sigmaringen and St. John of Leonessa
Giovanni Battista Tiepolo

Pope, the local Bishop, or a Catholic mob. His cruel drowning, which mocked his views on baptism, was perpetrated by dissenting Protestants.

The Protestants of Zurich believed in infant baptism while rejecting all other Catholic beliefs. And they allowed absolutely no dissenting from their own dissenting from Catholicism. Felix Mantz was the first Protestant martyred by other Protestants. Heretics killing other heretics for not conforming to their heresy captures the chaos, intellectual dissonance, and cultural confusion in some regions of sixteenth and seventeenth century Europe. This total meltdown is known as the Reformation. Today's saint, Fidelis of Sigmaringen, walked right into this still-raging storm of violence in the early seventeenth century, suffering a fate essentially similar to the Protestant martyr Felix Mantz, though for exactly contrary reasons.

Its very existence challenged by Protestantism, Counter-Reformation Catholicism swelled like a great ocean, lifting up a sea of scholars, monks, abbots, nuns, priests, and bishops who overwhelmed Europe with their teaching and witness to the perennial truths of Jesus Christ. Saint Fidelis was just one priest-monk among that great tide of the Counter-Reformation, but he was one who became a martyr. He was born as Mark Roy in the town of Sigmaringen in Prussia, in Northern Germany, and raised in the Faith. He earned a doctorate in philosophy in 1603 and degrees in civil and canon law in 1611, yet he became disillusioned with his career in law. He had always been an exceptionally ardent Catholic, so he entered the Capuchin Order and was ordained a priest in his thirties. He took the religious name of "faithful"—in Latin, "Fidelis." Fidelis was intelligent, disciplined, and ascetic. His abundant human and spiritual gifts were amplified and sharpened when put in the service of the King of Kings, and he rose to important positions of leadership within the Capuchin Order.

Having become locally well known for his fervor and holiness, Father Fidelis was appointed by the Congregation for the Propagation of the Faith in Rome to preach, teach, and write in present day Switzerland, with the goal of exhorting the people to return to the embrace of the Mother Church which had given them birth. Father Fidelis desired martyrdom, and it came for him soon enough. In Switzerland, his zeal and example brought some prominent Calvinists back to the true Faith. This made him an official enemy of the Calvinists who controlled much of that land.

One day, when traveling between two towns where he was preaching and saying Mass, Fidelis was confronted along the road by Calvinist soldiers led by a minister. Fidelis had recently caused an uproar in a nearby town and had barely escaped with his life. The soldiers knew exactly who was before them. They demanded that he abandon his Faith. Fidelis answered, "I was sent to rebuke you, not to embrace your heresy. The Catholic religion is the faith of all ages, I do not fear death." His skull was then cracked open with the butt of a sword, his body punctured with stabs, and his left leg hacked off in retribution for the numerous journeys he had made into Protestant territory. Saint Fidelis died at the age of forty-five, ten years after entering religious life. He was canonized in 1746. Over three hundred miracles were attributed to his intercession during his canonization process. Saint Fidelis was faithful in life and continues to intercede faithfully in death.

Saint Fidelis, through your intercession before the throne of God, we ask you to fortify all teachers and preachers of the faith to remain faithful to the truth, even to the point of embarrassment, inconvenience, suffering, and death to self.

APRIL

April 25: Saint Mark, Evangelist
c. First Century
Feast; Liturgical Color: Red
<u>*Patron Saint of lions, lawyers, Venice, interpreters, and prisoners*</u>

He chronicled what the first Pope witnessed

John's Gospel offers the reader this brief post-Resurrection scene: "Simon Peter said to them, 'I am going fishing.' They said to him, 'We will go with you.' They went out and got into the boat…" (Jn 21:3). The flock followed where Peter led. How easily Saint Peter moves to the fore in the Acts of the Apostles. How effortlessly he speaks for the entire Community of Faith. Saint Peter even leaves the running of the Church in Jerusalem to Saint James to show that he is not bound to one city or community. Instead, Peter walks toward the widest horizon of evangelization, the capital of the world—Rome. Traitor Peter becomes Pope Peter.

Peter was, of course, a simple fisherman. It is more interesting to note that he did not remain a simple fisherman. He grew. He matured. He led. And leaders don't have followers as much as joiners. Saint Mark, whom we commemorate today, was one of the most significant of the many joiners who uprooted themselves to join Peter in his dangerous adventure of founding the Church. Nothing is known for certain of Mark's origins or his youth. He is not mentioned in the Gospel that bears his name and only the faintest biographical sketch is possible. What is known is that Mark left his homeland in Palestine to follow first Saint Paul, and later, Saint Peter. Mark sailed dangerous seas in primitive boats. He walked long stretches through desolate lands. He tried to convince hardened pagans and skeptical Romans that the Gospel message was true. The words of the Acts of the Apostles, the letters of Saint Paul, and the First Letter of Saint Peter all put dots on the large map of Mark's life. Many blank spaces, however, still lay in between. Mark is traveling with Paul in Asia Minor, then he's with Barnabas on a boat over here, then he's with someone else over there, and then he disappears for a number of years. The scattered evidence ends, however, with clear testimony that Mark joined Peter in Rome. In Peter's first letter, written from the city of his death to the

Church in Asia Minor, Pope Peter sends greetings on Mark's behalf and refers to him as "my son"(1 Pt 5:13).

Saint Mark is, of course, best known as the author of a Gospel. Like Saint Luke and Saint Paul, he was not one of the Twelve Apostles and so likely never met Jesus Christ in person. Scholars believe that the Gospel of Saint Mark relates the experiences of Saint Peter, Mark's mentor. Each Gospel has its own unique sources, emphases, and audiences. Mark writes for non-Jews who would be impressed by Christ's miracles more than His fulfillment of Old Testament prophecies. So in Mark's Gospel are found certain colorful details that suggest the writer was relating the words of an eye-witness. For example, in Mark 5:41 Jesus enters the home of Jairus, a synagogue leader whose daughter lay dead. Christ says to her, *"Talitha koum."* Mark then tells the reader what *"Talitha koum"* means, presumably because his readers did not speak Aramaic. No other Gospel includes this touching detail of the untranslated words coming from the mouth of Christ that day. Mark also places other Aramaic words on Christ's lips: *"Ephphatha," "Abba,"* and *"Hosanna."*

Peter was there when it happened. Peter heard the Lord speak. And Peter was getting old, in prison, or threatened with death. The Gospel he had repeated verbally so many thousands of times had to be written down to send to others, to preserve its accuracy, or to contradict counterfeit versions. And so the natural progression from oral to written history slowly occurred. The Gospel was spoken before it was a book, and the word has primacy over the book. Saint Mark the Evangelist preserved for all time the Word of God, Jesus Christ, by committing Peter's words to writing, thus ensuring that the eye-witness accounts of Christ's life did not just float away in the breeze. Once the Word was enshrined on papyrus, Saint Mark had accomplished his mission forever and always.

Saint Mark, you were a friend of the Apostles and shared their commitment to spreading the faith. From your home in Heaven, may you strengthen all those who lack the courage to live the Gospel message in their own lives so they can witness it to others.

APRIL

April 28: Saint Peter Chanel, Priest and Martyr
1803–1841
Optional Memorial; Liturgical Color: Red
Patron Saint of Oceania

Musumusu axed him to death for no reason at all

In Paris, just a few blocks down the Rue du Bac from the shrine of the Miraculous Medal, is a fine, imposing stone building. There are a lot of fine, imposing stone buildings in Paris, so from the outside this one is not exceptional. But once the visitor passes inside the complex of chapel, museum, dormitories, and garden, he understands what a venerable institution he is visiting—The Paris Foreign Mission Society. Approximately 4,500 missionaries went forth from this unique Society, mostly to Southeast Asia, to build the Church and preach the Gospel. From its beginnings in the seventeenth century until today, but most conspicuously in the nineteenth century, hundreds of priests and bishops from the Society were martyred, died violent deaths, or fell victim to tropical diseases. Of these, twenty-three Paris Foreign Missionaries are canonized saints. Other non-martyr French saints of the same era—Saint John Vianney, Saint Thérèse of Lisieux, Saint Catherine Laboure—together with the missionary martyrs, sparkle as the jewels in the crown of the vibrant Church of nineteenth-century France.

Today's saint, Peter Chanel, was just one such Frenchman who left the comfort and familiarity of home to become a daring and rugged missionary priest. Peter Chanel grew up in rural France working as a shepherd. While in school, he loved to read about French foreign missionaries and wanted to emulate them. So he decided, "I will become a missionary priest!" After seminary studies, Peter was ordained a diocesan priest and served in parishes. But a few years later, he became one of the founding members of the Society of Mary, the Marists. And as a Marist father, he voyaged on the high seas to at last fulfill his missionary dreams. He sailed to one of the most tiny, remote, and unknown islands in the South Pacific. In 1837 Father Peter Chanel stepped ashore the speck of volcanic rock called Futuna to preach there, for the very first time, the name of Jesus Christ.

APRIL

On unknown Futuna, Father Chanel gave his all, at first drip by drip and then all at once. A lay brother who was with him later said of Father Chanel, "Because of his labors, he was often burned by the heat of the sun and famished with hunger, and he would return home wet with perspiration and completely exhausted. Yet he always remained in good spirits, courageous and energetic…" His apostolic labors generated few converts, but there was some progress nonetheless. Like so many missionaries, Peter had to overcome the counter-witness given by fellow European Christians trading in the area who cared little about their religion. In 1841 when the local Chieftain's son asked to be baptized, the Chieftain sent his son-in-law, Musumusu, to stop the conversion. A fight within the family ensued. Musumusu then went to Father Chanel's home and clubbed the priest with an axe until his blood puddled in the dirt. Father Peter was not yet forty years old when his missionary dream was fulfilled in martyrdom, giving Oceania its patron saint.

The island of Futuna, in which our saint had such mixed success, converted completely and totally a few years after Saint Peter's martyrdom. Musumusu himself repented of his crime and was baptized. The island is, even in modern times, almost one hundred percent Catholic. An impressive church is the heart and center of every small town. Saint Peter Chanel's body now rests in a large Basilica in the city of Poi. The beauty and smell of tropical flowers always adorn the church. And on the night of April 27, the vigil of his Feast Day, hundreds of Futunians sleep outside the Basilica waiting for the festivities of their saint's feast day to begin the next morning. The brief life and sudden death of Saint Peter Chanel is powerful proof of how the blood of the martyrs waters the seeds of the Church. One sows, another reaps, and still another enjoys the harvest.

Saint Peter Chanel, by your suffering and death, you converted a people. You were fearless in adventuring far from home to preach the Gospel. May your blood, spilled so long ago, continue to infuse all missionaries with courage and perseverance in their labors.

APRIL

April 28: Saint Louis Grignion de Montfort, Priest
1673–1716
Optional Memorial; Liturgical Color: White
<u>*Patron Saint of preachers*</u>

Intensely in love with God, his flame burned hot but not long

The English writer Graham Greene grew up Anglican with the typical anti-Catholic biases of his twentieth-century generation. One of those biases firmly held that Catholics worshipped the Virgin Mary and thus deflected toward Christ's mother the glory due to Him alone. But when Greene started dating an educated Catholic girl, she taught him that Catholics rendered *latria* (worship) to God, *dulia* (praise) to the saints, and *hyperdulia* (an abundance of praise) to Mary. It made sense. Worship is given to God alone. Praise is given to the saints. And Mary is rendered a unique intensity of praise in recognition of her unique role in salvation history. Graham was convinced. For these and other reasons, he entered the Church. He went on to become a well-known novelist on Catholic themes, in part because a teenage girl he once dated knew some basic theology.

Throughout the centuries since the Reformation, Catholics have been accused of granting to Mary what is due only to God. This false accusation is more apparent than real. But its appearance sometimes even bothers Catholics. As a young man, the future Pope Saint John Paul II wondered whether he gave Mary too central a role in his devotions, prayer, and reading. But the writings of today's saint, Louis de Montfort, helped the young Pole place Marian devotion in its wider theological context. Pope Saint John Paul II routinely gave thanks to Saint Louis de Montfort's book, *True Devotion to Mary*, for helping him develop a more mature Marian spirituality. The Pope even borrowed from de Montfort the Latin *Totus Tuus* as his papal motto. De Montfort had written to the Virgin, "I am all yours, and all that is mine belongs to you." When we honor Mary, Mary honors God along with us.

Louis Grignion de Montfort was never not in love with God. He was one of eighteen children born to his parents. Eleven of them are saints—Louis and ten of his siblings who died as babies shortly after their baptisms. Even as a child, Louis was devoted to prayer before the Blessed Sacrament. He studied under the Jesuits as a teen

APRIL

ST. LOUIS DE MONTFORT
April 28

"Mary has produced, together with the Holy Ghost, the greatest thing which has been or ever will be—a God-Man; and she will consequently produce the greatest saints that there will be in the end of time."

APRIL

and then attended theology courses at St. Sulpice in Paris. He was ordained a priest at the age of twenty-seven. He at first wanted to become a missionary, like so many ardent French priests of his time. But a spiritual director advised against it, and Louis became a hospital chaplain, preached missions, and served as a confessor. Father Louis was interpersonally awkward and ardent to the point of making others uncomfortable, all of which confined his priestly ministry to non-traditional forums. He also lived radical poverty, owning nothing, carrying no money, and even abandoning his family name, Grignion, to be known only by his town, Montfort.

Louis de Montfort's intense devotional life, theatrical preaching style, moral uprightness, and visions of Mary, the angels and satan, were interpreted as holy foolishness by many in the Church who wished him ill. The Jansenists, an ultra-rigorist branch of the French Church, particularly despised his preaching on God's love and mercy. Saint Louis' itinerant life ended due to physical exhaustion at the young age of forty-three. He practiced such extreme physical penances that his body was well prepared for the grave when he died. He was a priest only sixteen years. It is possible that his life and writings did more good for future ages than they did for his own. His writings on Mary, in particular, were rediscovered and published in the nineteenth century, leading to his canonization in 1947 and to his wide fame in the Church. Our saint died with a statue of the Virgin Mary in one arm and a crucifix given him by the Pope in the other arm. He felt attacked by the devil in his last agony and yelled at him, "You attack me in vain. I stand between Jesus and Mary. I have finished my course. I shall sin no more." He was buried, per his request, under an altar dedicated to his Lady...to Our Lady.

Saint Louis de Montfort, we ask your intercession before God in Heaven to inflame in all hearts a fire that burns like yours with love for the Holy Trinity. Help all who read your works to profit from their wisdom and so grow closer to God's mother.

APRIL

April 29: Saint Catherine of Siena, Virgin and Doctor
1347–1380
Memorial; Liturgical Color: White
Patron Saint of Italy, Europe, and fire prevention

Her frightening intensity prayed the popes back to Rome

Saint Peter was not martyred in Frankfurt, Germany; Alexandria, Egypt; or Jerusalem. He could have been. God, in His Providence, wanted Saint Peter's blood to spill on Roman soil, so that His One, Holy, Catholic, and Apostolic Church would drive its roots into the ground of the then capital of the world. This does not mean that Catholicism is bound to St. Peter's Basilica and Rome in the same way that Judaism was bound to the temple and Jerusalem. Rome does not have the same theological significance for Catholics as Jerusalem does for Jews, nor is Rome the successor of Jerusalem. Rome is not a holy city like Mecca is for the Muslims. The primacy of the Pope over the universal Church is based on his being the successor of Saint Peter. This is an indisputable historical fact. However, the Petrine ministry is one thing, and where it is exercised is another. The location of the Petrine ministry has never had the same theological weight as the ministry itself. Peter, yes. Always. Rome, yes. So far. Mostly.

Today's saint was a Third Order Dominican, a mystic, a contemplative, and an ascetic who used secretaries to compose her letters, because she could not read or write until the last few years of her life. Yet for all of her interior distance from the world and its concerns, Saint Catherine of Siena threw herself at the feet of the Pope, then reigning in Avignon, and begged him to return to Rome. The "Babylonian Captivity" of the papacy in Avignon had gone on for almost seven decades and caused grave scandal. The move to Avignon was not due to an irreversible cultural shift such as a Muslim conquest or a decimating plague. The popes did not abandon Rome because it was a carcass. The transfer of the papal court to Avignon, a city within the Papal States, was the result of politics.

It is not often that a single person can effect the course of history as much as a battle, a treaty, or a Council does. Incredibly, though,

APRIL

Saint Catherine of Siena's efforts to return the papacy to Rome were successful. She wrote so powerfully, spoke so passionately, and exuded such intense holiness that the Pope was overwhelmed. She also seemed to have prophetic powers, even knowing what the Pope was thinking or had previously thought. She was frighteningly intense and could not be ignored. Thus, sixty-seven years of seven French Popes ruling far from Rome ended. In 1376, Pope Gregory XI finally abandoned Avignon and followed in the footsteps of so many medievals—he went on pilgrimage to the tomb of St. Peter. And he stayed. The eternal city was a widow no longer.

Saint Catherine was born the twenty-fourth of twenty-five children in a pious family imbued with the love of God. She eagerly drank in all that her parents poured out. She went for true "gold" early in life. She practiced extreme penances, eating only bread and raw vegetables and drinking only water for her entire adult life. She conversed with God, experienced ecstasies and visions, and dictated hundreds of letters, books and reflections filled with the

St. Catherine of Siena

most profound spiritual and theological insights. In 1970 she was the first layperson, and first woman, to be made a Doctor of the Church, in recognition of her profound mystical theology. Catherine died at the age of thirty-three, worn out by penances, travel, and the burden of her involvement in so many pressing ecclesial affairs. She was canonized in 1461. Her body lies under the main altar of the Dominican Church of Santa Maria sopra Minerva in Rome. Her mummified head is found in her native Siena.

APRIL

Saint Catherine of Siena, your love of God was expressed in so many vibrant ways and in a fervent love of His Church. We seek your powerful intercession from your exalted place in heaven to make all Catholics more ardent in their love of the Trinity, of the Passion, and of the Papacy.

April 30: Saint Pius V, Pope
1504–1572
Optional Memorial; Liturgical Color: White
Patron Saint of the Congregation for the Doctrine of the Faith

One Shepherd, one flock, one Lord, one Church

Saint Pius V is buried in the Sistine Chapel, but not "that" Sistine Chapel. His body lies in a glass coffin in the stunning, baroque Sistine Chapel of the Basilica of Saint Mary Major in Rome. He is not far from other luminaries: the master artist Gianlorenzo Bernini is buried unassumingly in the floor nearby, and Saint Jerome's remains can be found in a porphyry tomb under the main altar. Saint Pius V was not born a pope, of course. He was from a poor but noble family in Northern Italy and baptized Antonio Ghislieri. He entered the Dominican Order as a teenager and quickly rose to positions of authority and responsibility due to his intelligence, discipline, unassailable purity of life, and defense of the Church.

He was elected Pope in 1566. The Council of Trent had just concluded. The Counter-Reformation was so new it did not even have a name. The Muslim Turks were invading Europe from the East. Protestants occupied chunks of Northern Europe and were cracking the unity of the Church in France. In a truncated papacy of six years and four months, Saint Pius V rose to all of these challenges and more, leaving an enduring legacy disproportionate to his brief reign.

Our saint marshalled the coalition of Catholic princes and monarchs who defeated the Turks at the Battle of Lepanto in 1571. A loss would have opened the front door of Europe for Muslims to walk right in and make it their home. In 1570, Pope Pius V excommunicated Queen Elizabeth I of England for heresy and schism, called her a pretender to the throne, and forbade Catholics to obey her. This led the Queen to seek the blood of English Catholics for treason. As momentous as these events were, and they each cast long and dark historical shadows, it was specifically as a churchman that Saint Pius V did his best work. He personally lived the reforms he expected of the Church as a whole, and he implemented those reforms first in the city of Rome itself, among his own ecclesial court and among his own people.

The Council of Trent met intermittently between 1545–1563. It was arguably the most successful Council in the history of the Church. Trent introduced numerous reforms that have long since been accepted as normative Church practice: a bishop must live in his diocese, priestly formation must occur in a seminary, the Mass must be said using a uniform language and ritual, a catechism must be published and its teachings learned by all, and religious and priests cannot easily skip from one diocese to another. The Council also clarified technical, and not so technical, questions of Catholic theology in the face of Protestant challenges. The Council's documents were not put on a shelf to gather dust. Trent's immense treasure house of doctrinal, liturgical, and disciplinary reforms were implemented, fully and forcefully, over many succeeding decades. This was due to the perseverance and vision of many Counter-Reformation bishops, priests, nuns, and scholars, beginning with Pope Saint Pius V himself.

Saint Pius V's tomb in the Sistine Chapel of Rome's St. Mary Major Basilica

Pope Saint Pius V is viewed historically as a true icon of orthodoxy (correct doctrine) and also of orthopraxy (correct practice). It is an unfortunate truism of modernity that religious faith, submission to religious truth, or trust in a prior intellectual inheritance (as opposed to personal discovery of "truth") are limiting forces which stunt personal growth, shield the believer from reality, or block more daring inquiry. A more honest perspective disproves these snide conclusions. Doubt, refusal, or negation are not necessarily open-minded pathways to discovery. It is acceptance, affirmation, and faith that open the mind to the widest horizons. It is "Yes," not "No," that leads to more complex and demanding relationships, including with God Himself. The orthodox believer makes no *a priori* decision to shut his eyes to the fullness of reality, in contrast to the atheist. The believer is open, truly open, to diverse arguments and to diverse experiences.

Defenders of orthodoxy, like Saint Pius V, have far more complex understandings of human anthropology and religion than commonly acknowledged. Conservatives are more intuitive anthropologists than liberals. They know how fragile truth can be when under pressure, and they take their job to protect it with utmost seriousness. Saint Pius V was the Pope, or Father, of a universal family. He protected the family's unity with all his considerable skills and virtues, and left a highly united, disciplined Church as his legacy.

Saint Pius V, your dedication to the truth showed itself in your pristine holiness, unity of life, and defense of doctrine. From your home in heaven, assist all theologians and leaders of the Church to be as concerned as you were for the unity of God's family on earth.

MAY

The Queen of May

MAY

May 1: Saint Joseph the Worker
Optional Memorial; Liturgical Color: White
<u>*Patron Saint of workers*</u>

God wanted a working man to father Jesus

Besides the Virgin Mary, there are just two saints who have more than one feast day dedicated to their honor on the Church's universal calendar: Saint John the Baptist and Saint Joseph. Pope Pius XII instituted today's feast in 1955 in direct response to the surge of atheistic communism in the decades after World War II. Communism at that time was not so clearly understood as the dehumanizing, anti-man, politically corrupt, and economically anemic system that it later revealed itself to be. Communism, after all, had helped defeat fascism in Germany and Italy, so it was understood as a liberating force, not an oppressive one, in some countries. May 1, or May Day, was the day of the worker in communist lands: a day of rest, of triumphant militaristic parades, and of pride in all that communism had accomplished, supposedly, for the proletariat.

Keen observers, including many Catholic intellectuals, Pope Pius XII, and one future Pope then serving as a priest in Poland, knew better. They had already, intellectually, torn the mask from the true face of communism. Part of the Church's response to the communist appeal to workers was to exalt Saint Joseph the Worker on May 1 as a Catholic alternative to May Day. Not only was Saint Joseph to be understood, then, as the husband of Mary and the foster father of Jesus, but also as the patron of labor. He was the carpenter, the working man, who taught his God-Son how to swing a hammer and run a planer over a rugged plank.

Pius XII's exaltation of Saint Joseph the Worker was an attractive idea. Saint Joseph was a true icon of human labor in contrast to the rough factory worker in an industrial plant in Leningrad or the tanned farm hand threshing hay under the Ukrainian sun. Saint Joseph did not have his fist raised in anger at the capitalist oppressors of Nazareth. He was not leading a mob to burn down his boss's house. Saint Joseph worked like a normal person worked. He was quiet about it. He did his duty. He provided his family with food and shelter. He didn't see injustice lurking behind every corner.

He most likely made excellent furniture and received a fair wage for his handiwork.

Work, from a Catholic perspective, is a source of dignity. It has to be done. A life of pure leisure is no life at all. Work and want and trying times are required ingredients in the recipe for a mature, responsible adult. No work, no adult. Work itself is not pure punishment. The onerous nature of work is one of the effects of original sin, though it was not so in the beginning. Work became a burden due to the sin of our first parents. What is the theology behind this? God the Father worked and God the Son worked. When man works, then, he is participating in God's own work. Subduing the earth is one of God's original commandments to man. And subduing the earth cannot come about except through work of one kind or another.

It has been observed that the dash (–) on a tombstone is far more important than the years that are on each side of it. What happened in the time of that dash is more important than one's date of birth or death. For most people that dash denotes work. Mankind works. All the time. And the will of God for us cannot be found outside of what we spend most of our life doing. If that were the case, then we wouldn't have much of a religion. God is found in our work. So if we do it well, we give him glory, and if we do it poorly, we offer him a shoddy sacrifice. The earth becomes our altar when our daily work is our daily offering. Constant, daily work was good enough for Saint Joseph and for the Son of God. So it is good enough for all of God's children as well. Work is a pathway to holiness, and Saint Joseph the Worker stands by our side to encourage us toward the reward that our daily sweat and labor will earn.

Saint Joseph the Worker, inspire all laborers of mind or body to work for their daily bread as much as for your glorification. May we work well to both perfect us and to make us participants in completing the creation begun in Genesis.

MAY

May 2: Saint Athanasius, Bishop and Doctor
c. 295–373
Memorial; Liturgical Color: White
<u>*Patron Saint of theologians*</u>

A fiery Egyptian saves the Trinity

The First Sunday of Advent of 2011 introduced to the faithful a new liturgical translation of the Mass in many English-speaking countries. The new translation had been many years in the making and had gone through numerous drafts and revisions. Of the many noticeable changes, some of the most extensive were made to the Nicene Creed. The phrase "one in being with the Father" was changed to "consubstantial with the Father." This caused confusion and discomfort for some, as "consubstantial" was not a familiar English word and sounded more appropriate to the realm of mathematics. But "consubstantial" had a long historical and theological pedigree supporting it. Its noticeable use in the newly translated Creed, and the curiosity it provoked, was also a distant homage to today's saint, Athanasius. He fought for, and suffered for, this one word.

Saint Athanasius was the sturdiest pillar of orthodoxy in the Patristic age. He was born to Christian parents in Egypt, raised in the faith, and mentored in his youth by the Bishop of Alexandria, whom he accompanied to the Council of Nicea. He later became the Bishop of Alexandria for forty-five contentious years and was exiled five times, some of them difficult, dangerous, and prolonged absences. He lived a colorful life at the very heart of the theological controversies of the fourth century. Athanasius, while still young, played an important role at the Council of Nicea in promoting the non-biblical, Greek word, *homoousion*, to describe Christ's relationship with God the Father. The Western Church then translated *homoousion* as *consubstantialis* for its Latin Creed. Hence the English word "consubstantial."

To say that Christ is "consubstantial" with the Father is to say that He is not one in person, one in mind, or one in will with the Father. He is distinct from the Father in His personhood, His mind, and His will. But Christ is entirely united to the Father in His substance, or nature. That is, Christ is God from God in the same way that

MAY

ST. ATHANASIUS
May 2

"Death has become like a tyrant who has been completely conquered by the legitimate monarch; bound hand and foot the passers-by sneer at him, hitting him and abusing him, no longer afraid of his cruelty and rage, because of the king who has conquered him."

light is from light or, to use the probable original analogy from that pre-electrified era, Christ is God from God and flame from flame. A wick carries a new flame away from its source, to burn the same or hotter somewhere else, without diminishing its "parent" fire. One source, two flames, generating heat and light in different places for different people.

Christ did not become God sometime after He was born of the Virgin Mary. He did not develop into God as a teenager. Nor was He bestowed with divine powers in some pivotal event. He was a baby God, a teen God, and an adult God because He was always God. Nor was His God nature a mere cloak under which was hidden a human self. Jesus Christ was fully human, of course, but also fully divine, and these two natures were united in one complex person. Most of the Church's finer Christological definitions were destined to be clarified at later Councils. The first two Councils, Nicea (325 A.D) and Constantinople (381 A.D.) were concerned with understanding and defining the Trinity first. Once Trinitarian definitions were worked out, later fifth-century Councils would address more fully the nature of Christ Himself.

Before delving into what Christ did, it was necessary to establish who He was. His *being* preceded His *doing*. Saint Athanasius' theological contributions to defining, for ever and all time, the metaphysical significance of the Incarnation is now taken for granted. But without this correct understanding, Christmas would be just a historic anniversary of an important birth, like that of Julius Caesar or other greats of history. But Christmas is Christmas because Christ was God from the start. Theology is not just a pillow on which the Church rests, of course, so the theology of the Trinity and of Christ has been greatly enriched since the Patristic age, most notably by an emphasis on the Cross as the fullness of the self-emptying that began with the Incarnation. Saint Athanasius was without equal in defining and defending the Church's dogma on the true nature of the Trinity. And for that immeasurable contribution he is owed an immense debt of gratitude by all the Church.

Saint Athanasius, your perseverance in combating false teaching cost you comfort and security. May your example and intercession assist all teachers to lead others to reflect more fruitfully on the truths and mysteries of our Faith.

May 3: Saints Philip and James, Apostles
First Century
Feast; Liturgical Color: Red
Patron Saint of hatmakers and pastry chefs (Philip) and pharmacists (James)

The smaller the town the bigger the man

The popes follow one another chronologically just like the presidents of the United States. One after another, after another, each inheriting the powers and responsibilities of his office. President John F. Kennedy followed President Dwight D. Eisenhower, just as Pope Saint John Paul II followed The Venerable Pope John Paul I. But there is a difference. Jesus' placing of Saint Peter as the symbolic and jurisdictional head of the universal Church is, of course, more significant than the popular election of a political leader. The papacy is also different in that every pope is, theologically speaking, the "direct successor" of Saint Peter, the first pope. From this perspective, every pope after Saint Peter is a second pope. So, for example, the two hundredth pope, chronologically, was still the second pope, theologically. No president would claim he is the direct successor of George Washington. He is the successor of his predecessor. Theological truths transcend space and time, since their source, God, exists outside of space and time.

The Office of St. Peter is theologically guaranteed by the easy-to-find, on-the-surface-of-the-text words of Christ telling Saint Peter that he is the rock upon which He will build His Church. Today's Pope, and every pope, occupies that same office, is protected by that same divine guarantee, and immediately succeeds Saint Peter when he is chosen by the Holy Spirit to occupy his chair.

What pertains to the Office of the Bishop of Rome also pertains to the Office of the Twelve Apostles. Today's saints, Philip and James, were called by name by Christ Himself. And after being called, they took the step that many who are called never take. They followed! The Twelve walked at Christ's side on dusty trails during His years of public ministry. They ate and drank with Him by the fire. They slept under the cold desert sky with Him. And Jesus looked right into their eyes, and only their eyes, and spoke directly to their faces, and only their faces, when He said on a Thursday night that was deeply holy, "Do this in memory of me." And then they did that, and many other things besides, in memory of Him, for the rest of their lives.

The four marks of the true Church are proof of its authenticity. "One, Holy, Catholic, and Apostolic" are the trademark stamp of the true Church, proving it is the Church founded by Jesus Christ. No other ecclesial community bears this trademark, and none except the Orthodox even claims to bear it. The mark of "One" means the Church is visibly one in spite of its many tongues, nations, classes, and races. The Church is one in her doctrine, her Sacraments, and her hierarchy. This oneness is not theoretical. It is tangible, real, and identifiable even to those without a doctorate in theology. This one, Christ-founded Church began with twelve followers who gathered as one around Jesus. These Twelve eventually appointed their own successors, who then, in turn, appointed successors, and so on through the centuries down to the present.

The universal college of bishops, the successor body to the Twelve Apostles, is the means by which the Oneness, or unity, of the Church is expressed, protected, and guaranteed. Bishops are not a secondary attribute or development of Christianity. They are embedded into and conjoined with the Word of God in one complex reality. They are not an outside source of authority external to Scripture. There simply would be no Scripture without that pre-existing authority which nurtured and developed it. The Church was the incubator of the New Testament.

Not much is known with certainty about the Apostles Philip and James, apart from their names and some few references in the New Testament. Saint James, commonly called the "Less" due perhaps to his short stature, was probably the cousin of Jesus. Saint Philip was from tiny Bethsaida in Galilee. After he received the Holy Spirit at Pentecost, he descended the stairs of the Upper Room and just kept walking into the darkness, his later life and labors unknown to history. More than having specific details about their later Christian exploits, it is more critical to know that Philip and James, and all the Apostles, are the sheet of bedrock into which the nascent Church sunk her deepest pillars and upon whose sturdy foundation the Church's great weight still rests. Philip and James' theological legacy continues today in every Bishop who teaches, sanctifies, and governs the baptized people of God.

Saints Philip and James, your hidden witness to Christ is less well-known than that of other Apostles, but is eloquent testimony to your quiet fidelity to building the Church after the Ascension. From your exalted place in Heaven, intercede for all who seek your assistance.

May 10: Saint Damien de Veuster of Moloka'i, Priest (U.S.A.)
1840–1889
Optional Memorial; Liturgical Color: White
Patron Saint of those suffering leprosy

A joyful celibate brings hope and dignity to the walking dead

It is often just one decision that releases the bolt, opening the door to a new life. The first step down a new road of a thousand smaller steps begins with one choice—to board the ship or to stand on the dock, to accept the marriage proposal or to wait for another, to sign the document or to leave it blank. Without that first choice, a different life would have been lived. Everyone, at some point, stands at this crossroad. But an impulse must be obeyed or rejected for untold other events, decisions, and influences to begin to unwind. This is one of the mysteries of life, how so much depends on one brief moment.

Young Jozef De Veuster (Damien was his religious name), growing up in a large family in rural Belgium, could never have imagined where and how his life would end. He was most likely going to follow the path of most other young men of his time and place—get married, have a family, go to Mass on Sunday, and take over the family farm. But an older brother was a priest, and two sisters were nuns, so a religious vocation was always a possibility. Damien eventually responded to the Lord's call and his own impulse toward religious life and entered the Congregation of the Sacred Hearts of Jesus and Mary, just as his brother did before him. But just as his brother, Father Pamphile, was slated to leave for Hawai'i as a missionary, he had to abandon his voyage for health reasons. And thus a decision had to be made. A pivot point had arrived. Was Damien to replace his brother and go to Hawai'i or not? Leave family forever or stay home? Be a foreign missionary or stay among his own? Brother Damien walked the long plank upward and boarded the ship. He arrived in Honolulu in March 1864 and was ordained a priest in May. He would live his entire priestly life in Hawaiʻi. He never left the Hawaiʻian islands again.

Father Damien served in parishes for several years, learning to love his parishioners and being loved by them in return. Then, in 1873, the bishop asked for volunteers to go to an isolated leper colony on the island of Molokaʻi. Father Damien volunteered. For the next sixteen years, he dedicated himself without reserve to this exiled community. He carried out more than a "ministry of accompaniment." He accompanied, yes, but he also led, taught, inspired, and died to self. Father Damien's robust health and farm background made hard work natural. He enlarged a chapel and built a rectory, a road, a dock, and numerous cottages for the lepers. He showed the people how to farm, to raise cattle, and to sing (despite his diseased vocal cords), and to play instruments (despite his missing fingers).

He was a vital force walking in a living graveyard. Life on an isolated leper colony was psychologically difficult for everyone, even the priest. But Father Damien brought faith and human dignity to a depressed population alienated from family and society. He treated the sick and the dying—and everyone was sick and dying—with the dignity of children of God. A proper cemetery was organized, funeral Masses were said with the accompaniment of a choir, and solemn processions bore everyone to their final resting place. This was a far cry from the inhuman chaos that preceded his arrival.

Father Damien carried out all of his pastoral work with fatherly concern. He was there, after all, because he was a celibate priest. No married Protestant minister would have dared to place himself, his wife, and his children in such a dangerous situation, and none ever did. Like all good fathers, Father Damien was both joyful and demanding. He was open. He smiled. He cared. He scolded. His source of strength was not merely his solid foundation in human virtue but primarily his Catholic faith. Father Damien's love for the Mass, the Holy Eucharist, and the Virgin Mary deepened through the years. His greatest non-physical sufferings were the lack of a priest companion with whom he could converse and to whom he could confess his sins.

Father Damien contracted leprosy after eleven years in the colony. He personally never wrote to his mother with the news. But when the old widow in Belgium learned of her son's illness, she died of a broken heart. Father Damien lived five years with leprosy, continuing his priestly work, and died in 1889 at the age of forty-nine. He was canonized by Pope Benedict XVI in 2009 after two medical miracles were attributed to his divine intervention.

Saint Damien of Moloka'i, intercede on behalf of all fathers to make them ever more generous in serving without reserve the families they head, making your life not only a source of inspiration, but also of emulation, to all who know of your heroic generosity.

May 10: Saint John of Ávila, Priest and Doctor
1499-1569
Optional Memorial: Liturgical Color: White
Patron Saint of Andalusia Spain and Spanish clergy

His humble epitaph reads "I was a sower"

Some of the most passionate and daring missionaries stayed close to home. They never sailed the high seas or crossed a snow-capped mountain. Today's saint was one of them. He was an only child, and after his parents died, Fr. John sold his family property, travelled to Seville, cut all ties, and prepared to sail to New Spain (Mexico), one more wave in that surging missionary tide which crashed on Mexico's shores throughout the 1500s. But it was not to be. St. John of Ávila never walked up the ship's plank. He never crossed the ocean. While waiting for his ship in Seville, his skills as a preacher and catechist, and his obvious holiness, were noticed by the local bishop, who convinced him to preach, teach, and evangelize in Andalusia, in Spain's rugged south.

Saint John then spent himself crisscrossing a region that had only recently been conquered by the Spanish crown, and so was still populated by Spanish Muslims and Jews whose conversions to Catholicism were often more matters of expedience than religious conviction. In this newly opened mission field, our saint's broad, humanistic education perfectly matched the pastoral need. Father John harmonized orthodox theology, renaissance humanism, rigorous morality, and an insightful spirituality into a powerful synthesis which, when conveyed through his compelling preaching, moved his congregations to their very cores. As John migrated through the great cities of southern Spain - Seville, Córdoba, Granada – large numbers of the faithful followed him everywhere, eager to absorb every word that flowed from his mouth or pen.

People of every class, educational level, and depth of religious commitment found St. John fascinating. In his own lifetime he came to be known as "Master Ávila" for his dominance of the sacred sciences and his vigorous pastoral efforts. He converted, or led to deeper conversion, Saint John of God, founder of the Hospitaller Order, and Saint Francis Borgia, a future Master General of the Jesuits. He was a friend of Saint Ignatius of Loyola, founder of the Jesuits, and advised Saint Teresa of Ávila, foundress of the Discalced Carmelites. Despite these, and many other, personal connections to famous religious orders and their founders, St. John always remained a diocesan priest, not a religious order priest, something unusual for a priest of his era with such wide influence.

Saint John's erudition and solid virtues were further buttressed by his life of abject poverty and physical suffering. He was also part of that loud, pan-European cry for church reform that preceded the Council of Trent by decades. Saint John established several seminaries and colleges, provided spiritual direction to multitudes of laity, religious and seminarians, wrote a long spiritual treatise called *Audi filia* ("Listen daughter") and was invited by a bishop to attend the Council of Trent as his theological adviser, though illness prevented Saint John from making the journey.

John was declared Venerable in 1759, Blessed in 1893, and Saint in 1970. Proving that saints are always contemporary, he was declared a doctor of the Church by Pope Benedict XVI in 2012 after a petition from the Spanish episcopacy for such an honor was duly studied and approved by the Vatican. The Papal Bull declaring him a Doctor of the Church states: "The teaching of John of Ávila is outstanding for its quality and precision, and its breadth and depth, which were the fruit of methodical study and contemplation together with a profound experience of supernatural realities."

In his last few years, Saint John suffered acute physical pain and was largely confined to his humble home. Confinement allowed him to finally perfect his theological and spiritual writings and to correspond with those seeking his wise counsel. The esteemed Master Ávila, a true Man of La Mancha, died clutching a crucifix, surrounded by many disciples, on May 10, 1569.

Saint John of Ávila, your refined education, broad mind, and ardent love of God and Mary showed itself in all you did and said. May our lives likewise reflect our deepest Christian beliefs, inspiring our friends and families to live saintly perfection.

May 12: Saints Nereus and Achilleus, Martyrs
c. Early Second Century
Optional Memorial; Liturgical Color: Red

Roman soldiers made good martyrs

The earliest manuscript proving the existence of Roman Emperor Julius Caesar, a copy of one of his works, dates from the ninth century A.D. Caesar was stabbed to death in 44 B.C. So approximately nine hundred years separate the life of Caesar from the first tangible, physical, paper copy of one of his written works. The earliest manuscript describing Caesar, but not written by him, dates from after the ninth century, and so is even more removed from the man it describes. None of this means that Julius Caesar did not exist or that he did not compose the works attributed to him. First century B.C. Roman coins prove, unequivocally, that Julius Caesar existed.

No Roman coins prove the existence of today's martyrs. Instead, something thousands of times larger than a coin proves they existed. There's a church. In fact, there are two churches in Rome dedicated to Saints Nereus and Achilleus. These churches are not hard to find. You can touch their walls, open their doors, and sit in their pews. There is not one structure, much less two, in Rome or in any other city, dedicated to Julius Cesar. Even the exact location of his assassination is a matter of conjecture.

MAY

Christian martyrs in the colosseum

Gustave Doré

Almost nothing can be said with certainty regarding the lives and deaths of Nereus and Achilleus. There are conflicting traditions of when they lived, where they lived, and how they died. But...there are those churches. Two of them. In Rome. One is a fourth-century Basilica inside the Catacombs of Domitilla. The other, from the sixth century, was built on the site where an early Christian tradition says Saint Peter encountered Christ as Peter was abandoning Rome.

A stone is a valuable form of testimony. It is more permanent than paper. A stone doesn't easily deteriorate. A stone is heavy and remains where its builder placed it. Its location itself provides important clues. The stones of the two Roman churches dedicated to today's saints give powerful, if silent, testimony. The churches are planted in the earth like giant gravestones telling who can be found in or beneath them. Who would assume that the words etched into a gravestone were a lie? Who would think that a name carved into granite described no one? Who would imagine that the ground under a memorial was empty, holding no grave, no casket, no body? Only a fool would believe such things. But Christians are no fools.

An enormous death memorial, in the form of a church, was built by dedicated Christians in the fourth century in honor of today's saints. Nereus and Achilleus were likely soldiers who were executed for their belief in Jesus Christ. An official list of Roman martyrs from the fifth-century names, specifically, Nereus and Achilleus, and states, specifically, that they are buried in the Catacombs of St.

MAY

Domitilla. Pope Saint Gregory the Great, who reigned from 590–604, gave a homily, duly recorded and preserved, at the very tomb of Saints Nereus and Achilleus: "These saints before whose tomb we are assembled, despised the world and trampled it under their feet…" And more than one medieval manuscript records an ancient dedication to Nereus and Achilleus by Pope Damasus (366–384) attesting to their martyrdom for refusing to carry out military orders to kill Christians.

The relics of today's saints were transferred from their ancient underground Basilica in the catacombs to their "new" Church sometime in the sixth century. By the ninth century, the Basilica had been forgotten as wave after wave of invasion and plague and sack and turmoil decimated the Eternal City until it was a shadow of its imperial glory. But in 1874, a pioneering archaeologist named Giovanni de Rossi began excavating the Catacombs of Domitilla. In the ruins of a subterranean Basilica there, he found two pillars, one of which had the name "Achilleus" carved into it. De Rossi also discovered chunks of the very marble slab bearing the dedication of Pope Damasus to Nereus and Achilleus! This discovery proved the medieval manuscripts describing the dedication were accurate. The stones spoke. The faithful listened. The traditions are true. The Church preserved its sacred history, and today the great tradition of honoring those who shed their blood for Christ perdures.

Saints Nereus and Achilleus, we know little about you, except the most important things—that you lived, that you converted, and that you chose to not continue living rather than to deny your belief in Christ. We know these things, and they are enough. Pray for us.

May 12: Saint Pancras, Martyr
Third Century
Optional Memorial; Liturgical Color: Red
Patron Saint of children, jobs, and health

A fatherless teen discovers a treasure worth life itself

In the late 500s, Pope Saint Gregory the Great appointed monks to staff a small church in Rome, already almost three hundred years old, which was dedicated to Saint Pancras. In 597 the same Pope

MAY

Gregory sent Saint Augustine of Canterbury on a missionary journey to England, and Augustine copied his Roman mentor and established a church in honor of Saint Pancras. About sixty years after Augustine, a different pope sent relics of Saint Pancras to England. This further spread devotion to this boy martyr, until a total of six ancient churches were dedicated to Saint Pancras in England alone, including the oldest church still used for Christian worship in that old country.

Little is known with certainty about the life of Saint Pancras, but the essential facts are sufficient cause for admiration. Pancras was an orphan who traveled to Rome from the east in the company of his uncle. The pair converted to Christianity and then died for that conversion during the reign of Diocletian. Pancras was perhaps fourteen years old when he traded his earthly life for a better one in heaven. He likely became well known owing to his rare combination of youth and heroic witness. Our martyr was buried near a major Roman road, and a modest basilica was constructed over his tomb. The shrine and its catacombs became a popular pilgrimage destination, partly due to its healing bath, which was famous for its curative powers. The ravages of time and foreign armies degraded the shrine, but it was rebuilt several times over the centuries. In the seventeenth century, the Basilica of Saint Pancras was entrusted to the Discalced Carmelite Order, whose members still reside there today. Under the Basilica are extensive Roman catacombs, and a reliquary in the church contains the head of Saint Pancras. The rest of the saint's relics were scattered to the four winds by anti-Catholic armies who occupied the church and despoiled many of its treasures.

Moments of great danger for the Church are also moments of great grace. In her long history, the Church has passed through, and continues to live, many such dangerous, grace-filled times. Saint Pancras' times were precisely such. If he had stayed in his native land, he would likely have died of natural causes. But he went in search of something, perhaps wealth, fame, or family, in Rome, the big city, just as so many people search for the same in big cities today. But young Pancras found what he probably wasn't looking for—God. And his decision to become a Christian, perhaps through the influence of a friend or priest or aunt, quickly took a very serious turn. He was threatened with death if he did not burn incense to a false god. The boy stood fast. Like other more famous young martyrs, such as Saint Agnes, the idealism of youth provoked both admiration and fury in his persecutors, and he was taken beyond the walls of Rome to be decapitated.

Our culture and its pressures are not from God. They are human constructs. But our Church, which is an object of faith, *is* from God. The friction caused by the collision of culture and church damages individuals, parishes, and governments. Sparks fly. Heat is generated. Objects melt. At times, wars ensue. Today's martyr was an early victim to something far bigger than himself—the culture clash between a dying empire and a dawning religion. If he had gone to Rome just ten years later, Pancras would have lived in peace. Instead, Pancras and many others were executed, because they refused to bend to a leader who might die tomorrow in favor of a God who rose to life from a cold tomb.

Saint Pancras, you gave away your young life rather than offer worship to a false god. May your example inspire, and your intercession strengthen, all young people to put love of God above all else.

May 13: Our Lady of Fatima
1917
Optional Memorial; Liturgical Color: White

Like the moon's mellow glow, Mary reflects a greater light

The ancient Greco-Roman world that Christianity replaced was deeply devoted to the gods, not God. Its landscape was dotted with a thousand shrines, oracles, sacred caves, and holy mountains where the god of this and the goddess of that lived or lurked. And the pagan faithful—and they were faithful—trusted that someone among this government of gods could be petitioned for this need or lobbied for that favor: so that the battle would be won, the harvest plentiful, the illness brief, the baby a boy, or the sea calm for the voyage. This all made sense. Just as human nature was expressed in countless persons, so too would the divine nature be manifested in myriad gods and goddesses. Countless stars populated the blackness between earth and sun. So too did gods thicken the reality between the realm of the flesh and the realm of the spirit in ancient paganism.

Over a span of centuries, Christianity methodically and inexorably displaced this ancient worldview. The Church rolled slowly on, like a colossal glacier, from east to west and south to north, gathering, pushing, and budging everyone and everything to the margins as it carved a new landscape for a new people. Yet the old worldview, while theologically childish, had deeply human elements. It is natural to think that between man and god there would be sub-gods or something of the like. It is natural to imagine that a local god would have local concerns and give a local answer to local people. It is natural to presume that a high summit is holier than a flat prairie and that to visit it, to make a petition, and to leave an offering would merit more than to do nothing at all. Greco-Roman paganism expressed the deep, universal, religious impulse found in every culture.

Christianity built on the same human foundations as paganism, and it responded to the same human longings. But Christianity built on that sound foundation a solid house of revealed theological truth. And that truth revealed that the one God—omniscient, omnipresent, all powerful—expresses Himself through the tool of creation, though He Himself is not creation. Christian truth also revealed that God not only acts through secondary causes but is also approached through them. So bread and water become Christ's Body and Blood, water is blessed by a holy man and wets our foreheads when we mark ourselves with the cross, and certain men and women live so heroically the mystery of God in their lives that we call them saints. This constellation of saints has long replaced the confused, but understandable, pagan pantheon of old. Instead of a god of the sea, a god of war, and a god of rain, we have patron saints for sailors, soldiers, and farmers. We have saint intercessors for the mentally ill, for pregnant women, for impossible causes, and for a happy death. Catholicism has a saint for everything and for everyone, forming a more theologically satisfying worldview that nonetheless responds to the innate religious impulse of all men.

Today's Memorial celebration commemorates the greatest saint of all, Saint Mary, as she manifested herself to three humble children in the Portuguese village of Fatima in 1917. Our Lady, the only mother ever chosen by her son, appeared in a particular place, at a particular time, to a particular people, to satisfy a particular need. She spoke to the children deep theological truths about heaven, hell, and purgatory. She performed a publicly witnessed miracle that made the sun dance, asked for increased devotion to her Son Jesus Christ, and pleaded for reparation for the many sins committed against Him. A shrine was built in the Blessed Mother's honor at the site of her apparitions, which has welcomed millions and millions of pilgrims, including popes, over the decades. Our Lady is for the whole Church, of course, but she is closer to the faithful when she comes to them on their own terms—in their own tongue, skin, and dress, hovering over their own soil. There is one Mary, historically and theologically. There are many Marys, culturally and symbolically.

Pope Saint John Paul II was shot on the Feast of Our Lady of Fatima, May 13, 1981, in St. Peter's Square in Rome. He was grievously injured but survived. He later said that one hand pulled the trigger, but another hand guided the bullet. He went on pilgrimage to Fatima to give thanks for that saving hand. The bullet that penetrated his torso, and was removed by doctors, was placed into the silver crown of Our Lady of Fatima. It rests there today. We honor Mary for many graces, we petition her for many favors, and we thank her for many gifts—for the battle won, for the plentiful harvest, for the healthy baby, for the calm sea, and for the lives saved, dramatically, from an assassin, or mundanely, from everything else.

Our Lady of Fatima, your miraculous apparitions fill us with hope that you follow our concerns, intervene in our lives, and demand of us greater fidelity. May we heed your words and your warnings and carry out God's will with your own life as our example.

May 14: Saint Matthias, Apostle
First Century
Feast; Liturgical Color: Red
Patron Saint of alcoholics and tailors

The Twelve were deeply biblical—Judas had to be replaced

Conservative Muslims believe that any territory that was once settled and governed by the adherents of Mohammed pertains forever and always to the Caliphate. Once Islamic, always Islamic. To illustrate, it took many generations for the Islamic fist to finally loosen its grip on Spain. Yet despite the Muslim armies being pushed back into the waters of the Mediterranean in 1492, some strict modern followers of Mohammed still harbor dreams of former glories and hope that Al-Andalus (Muslim Spain) will one day re-emerge.

Catholicism harbors no such illusions of glory for formerly Catholic lands, but it does practice a theological form of

St. Matthias
Marco Pitteri

"Once Catholic, Always Catholic." Many Bishops who serve in the Roman Curia exercise no authority over a diocese. Auxiliary bishops likewise lack a territory. These two categories of bishops are thus given a "titular" episcopal see. It is a see in name, or title, only. The see is normally that of an ancient diocese whose existence ceased due to, typically, Muslim invasion. The custom of assigning "titular" sees to some bishops not only preserves the memory of lost peoples and dioceses, it also has some theological support. A bishop and his diocese are united, like spouses, in a marriage arranged in Rome. That's why a bishop wears a ring. And a diocese, once created, cannot remain a widow. A new bishop is always appointed to be wedded to it. A diocese must have a spouse, even if he is a long way from home in distance and time. Titular bishops succeed in the present, if only in name, the past bishops of now defunct dioceses.

The tradition that all bishops, beginning with the Apostles, must have successors is rooted not just in the early Church but in Judaism. The Twelve Apostles are more often referred to in the New Testament by their number than their names. They are, simply, "The Twelve." This custom is rooted in the twelve tribes who settled the land of Canaan after the Exodus from Egypt. These tribes were founded by the twelve sons of the Patriarch Jacob, later renamed Israel. It was inside of this Old Testament Jewish tradition that Jesus Christ acted when He chose twelve men upon whom to found His Church. Jesus specifically states that His followers will sit on twelve thrones judging the twelve tribes of Israel (Mt 19:28, Lk 22:30). And the Book of Revelation states that the names of the twelve tribes of Israel will be written on the gates of the Heavenly Jerusalem (Rv 21:12 ff).

It was fitting, then, when "The Twelve" were reduced to "The Eleven" after Judas' self murder, that the fullness of the biblical number had to be restored. And this is where today's saint steps out from the shadows to play his role in Christian history. The first chapter of the Acts of the Apostles, the great history book of the early Church, tells us that, after the Ascension, the eleven Apostles returned to Jerusalem. There, Peter "stood up among the believers" to tell them that someone who had "accompanied us during all the time that the Lord Jesus went in and out among us… must become a witness with us to his resurrection." Two names were proposed to replace Judas: Matthias and Joseph called Barsabbas. Then the Eleven prayed to the Lord to show them the way. They cast lots. Matthias was chosen. An Apostle, for the first time, had a successor. And, of equal significance, the appointment came from the group, or college, of Apostles, led by Peter. Thus was established, just days after Christ left the earth, a form of Church preservation and growth which would be repeated, and is still repeated, tens of thousand of times in Christian history.

The Church has placed the Feast of St. Matthias purposefully close to the Feast of the Ascension, just as his election in Acts occurred so soon after that event in the Bible. The Holy Spirit had yet to descend at Pentecost, and still the Church performed the will of God with authority in selecting Matthias. It was all there in the beginning. It is still here all around us. The miracle of the Church and her Apostles continues. It will always continue.

Saint Matthias, we beg your intercession from your powerful throne in the Heavenly Jerusalem, that you fortify all who govern your Church to emulate "The Twelve" in their wisdom, trust, prudence, and daring in leading and spreading the Faith.

May 15: Saint Isidore
c. 1080–1130
Optional Memorial (U.S.A.); Liturgical Color: White
Patron Saint of farmers and brick layers

Our daily duties are not a distraction from God's will

It would be wonderful to see in a church a marble statue of a nurse taking a patient's blood pressure. It would be edifying to see in a Basilica's bright stained glass a housewife standing fatigued at the ironing board, running the iron over her kids' shirts. And it would be marvelous to gaze in admiration at a well-executed painting of a factory worker pounding a piece of metal into shape with a hammer. Imagine if Catholic art presented these mundane scenes for contemplation in our churches, chapels, and shrines. Imagine kneeling before a bank of glowing candles and reflecting upon the everyday heroism of the lay vocation. We could light a small candle, step back, cross our hands, pause in silence, look at the layman in a suit at his desk in the mosaic before us, and whisper a prayer asking for his divine intercession to help us be a more charitable nurse, a more dedicated housewife, or a more honest worker.

There is nothing in the mind that is not first in the senses. So our churches inspire us, ideally, with their statues, stained glass, paintings, mosaics, floors, and tapestries. The images of the holy men and women of our long Catholic tradition typically show popes, bishops, priests, nuns, abbots, monks, friars, brothers, missionaries, and others, dressed in their religious habit and armed with the symbols of their office and their life. All of this is good. All of this is necessary. All of this is inspiring. Yet today's saint, Isidore, offers us a different pathway of holiness to consider—the broad and well-traveled pathway crowded with the Catholic laity on their way to work in the morning.

Saint Isidore was from Spain and was named in honor of Saint Isidore of Seville, a scholar, bishop, and Father of the Church who lived in the sixth and seventh centuries. The two Isidores could not be more different. Today's Saint Isidore is known in Spanish as "Labrador" or "the farm worker." He was not a scholar and probably had trouble reading. He was not ordained to Holy Orders but married and a father. He surely had calluses on his hands, a red, leathery neck burned by the sun, and a sore and twisted back for most of his life. He earned what little he had. No one gave it to him. He did not put food on his family's table by generating great thoughts or publishing profound books. And due to exhaustion he probably had no trouble sleeping at night.

Numerous legends of miracle working and holiness attest to Saint Isidore's influence on Spanish culture. In 1947 his partially incorrupt body was even put on public display to provoke prayers to bring a terrible Spanish drought to an end. Saint Isidore is the patron saint of Madrid and of numerous other towns, cities, and regions throughout the Iberian Peninsula and Latin America. Processions, Masses, fireworks, and public devotions render him homage on his feast day. Yet besides his dedication to working the land, few details of Saint Isidore's life are known with certainty.

Our religious faith cannot occupy only one sphere of our life, as if it were a hobby akin to building a ship in a bottle, flying a kite, or cultivating a garden. A real religion impacts everything. Even work. Especially work. We fulfill God's will in our daily lives—which are packed full of work—by doing our work well. We should do our work diligently and at a high professional level, because it is an offering to God first and foremost. In other words, bad work equals a bad offering. Work is the practical use and expression of the skills

ST. ISIDORE
May 15

*"St. Isidore, patron of farmers, pray for us.
St. Isidore, illustrious tiller of the soul, pray for us.
St. Isidore, model of laborers, pray for us.
St. Isidore, devoted to duty, pray for us.
St. Isidore, loaded down with the labors of the field, pray for us."*

God has loaned us for our earthly pilgrimage. To misuse those skills, to let them lie fallow, or to put them to ill use, is to bury a treasure in the ground. *"Ora et Labora"* is the Benedictine maxim. Prayer and Work. Yet work is prayer for the vast majority of the baptized.

Saint Isidore's life teaches us, indirectly, that God can convert an entire nation without ink or paper. A book might help, of course, but a religion of the Word is not the same as a religion of the Book, and Catholics are a people of the Word. Saint Isidore is the patron saint of farmers, day laborers, and brick layers. He is often shown wearing rough clothes, oxen leading him as he plows a furrow, with an angel at his side and a golden halo shining over him. A farmer saint. Why not?

Saint Isidore, your witness of dedicated and holy work is a model for all who earn their bread by the sweat of their brow. May your quiet and humble dedication to your lay vocation inspire all the baptized to see in "work well done" a source of dignity through which man participates in God's creative act.

May 18: Saint John I, Pope and Martyr
c. Late Fifth Century–526
Optional Memorial; Liturgical Color: Red

The pope is crushed in a secular vice by two worldly masters

The early Popes were Roman citizens who retained their birth or baptismal names upon being elected to the See of Peter. Their names perfectly reflect a flourishing Roman culture rather than the Christian subculture which was gradually budding and flowering in its midst. So there are Popes Clement, Linus, Anacletus, Sixtus, Victor, Callixtus, Urban, and Fabian. It sounds like a roll call of Roman senators in white togas seated on the marble benches of the Forum. It is not until 254 that Pope Stephen bears a name from the New Testament and not until 336 does Pope Mark honor an Evangelist.

Considering the centrality of Saints John the Evangelist and John the Baptist to the Christian story, it is surprising that five hundred years transpired before today's saint, Pope John I, so honored their memory. A pope is only called the "First" once there's a "Second." In 533 a man named Mercurius succeeded today's John as Bishop of Rome. Mercurius' birth name was so overtly pagan—honoring the Roman God Mercury—that he chose to honor his martyred predecessor John by adopting his same name. Mercurius thus initiated the venerable tradition of a pope adopting a new name upon his election. At the same time he also retroactively turned Pope John into Pope John I.

The flow of the early martyrs' blood had long since ceased by John I's election in 523. There was no emperor or court even left in Rome by 523 for barbarians to attack. The traditional date of the fall of the Western Roman Empire is 476. John I was, then, the pope of a declining, far western outpost of an empire whose central government had been in Constantinople for almost two hundred years by John I's election. Rome was fading.

The Empire's long, slow decline in Italy had created a vacuum. Rugged tribes of the North, including the Ostrogoths (Eastern Goths), poured south into the warm valleys and cultured towns of the Italian countryside and saturated Rome itself. The Ostrogoths had called the Italian peninsula home for so long that, by the sixth century, they were part Roman, part barbarian, and part Christian. Borderlands are always a mix. For complex historical reasons, the Ostrogoths and their Italian ruler, Theodoric, were Arians. Their prior isolation in Northern Europe had prohibited them from absorbing the teachings of the fourth-century Councils of Nicea and Constantinople. So the Ostrogoths were unaware that the Church had decisively rejected the Arian heresy, which held that Christ was *a* god, but not *the* God.

It was amidst these tense political and religious circumstances that poor Pope John I was placed in an impossible situation. John was caught between the Emperor Justin in remote Constantinople, who exercised significant control over Church discipline, and Theodoric, who was standing right at his side, breathing down his neck. Justin had issued an edict ordering the Arians, including the Ostrogoths in Italy, to surrender their churches to the Catholics. Theodoric would have none of it. He was as angry as a hornet. To him, it was the first step toward Constantinople reasserting its control over Italy, something the Ostrogoths would resist to the death. So Theodoric sent Pope John at the head of a large embassy of Roman dignitaries to Constantinople to demand that Justin withdraw the edict. Pope

John obediently went. He was greeted in the capital with elaborate ceremony and honored as head of the Church. But he could not, and did not, secure what Theodoric so desired. It was impossible. The edict was binding.

When Pope John and his party crossed the Adriatic Sea to return to Rome, they landed at Ravenna. Theodoric, who had heard of Pope John's failure to have the edict rescinded, imprisoned him. And there the Pope died, in Ravenna, perhaps of shock, perhaps of mistreatment. His blood did not run red like the martyrs of old, but he died a victim for Christ nonetheless, unable to simultaneously satisfy two powerful secular masters. John I's mortal remains were returned to Rome. In keeping with the custom for all popes since Pope Leo the Great (440–461), Pope John I was interred in the nave of the Constantinian Basilica of St. Peter. When the new St. Peter's was built in the sixteenth and seventeenth centuries, John's tomb did not surface nor did any epitaph. But Pope Saint John I is still there, somewhere, under the floor of St. Peter's, arms crossed, facing up, ring on his bony finger, vested in gold, miter crowning his head, as waves of tourists walk on the marble floor above him. He rests in peace, forgotten to but a few.

Pope Saint John I, your fidelity to your vocation as Pope led to your death. You were faithful in the face of threats from civil power but did not bend to its will. May all popes look to your example for inspiration in leading the Church.

May 20: Saint Bernardine of Siena, Priest
1380–1444
Optional Memorial; Liturgical Color: White
Patron Saint of advertising and gambling

A sensational preacher popularizes the Holy Name devotion

Saint Bernardine of Siena was the Billy Graham of his day. Graham was a well-known American evangelist who traveled ceaselessly from city to city preaching the good news of the Gospel over many decades. Yet while today's saint was certainly a roving evangelist, he was also much more. He was first and foremost vowed to poverty, chastity, and obedience as a Franciscan Friar. Saint Bernardine was also ordained into the one Priesthood of Jesus Christ by a successor of the Apostles. And he had received a long and complete theological and humanistic education before he ever opened his mouth in front of a crowd. He was even a doctor of canon law.

Fifteenth-century Italy was hot with reform of the Church. Ever since 1417 and the end of the Great Schism (an era of two and even three competing popes), talk of Church reform was on the lips of anyone who believed enough to care. Unfortunately, every effort to compel a bishop to live in his diocese, to form better educated priests, to purify indulgence selling, to streamline Church courts, to appoint holy bishops, to stop commerce in relics, and so on, was ignored or resisted. The roots of some weeds are tangled and ferocious. They cannot be pulled from the ground. The 1400s were a lost century for efforts to reform the Church. The popes tightened their grip on Church power so that no council would ever pry their fingers from the levers of ecclesial governance. The needed reforms would have to wait until the immensely successful Council of Trent in the mid-sixteenth century. But it was too late by then. Father Martin Luther and others had been tired of waiting. The Reformation began in 1517, one hundred years after the Great Schism ended. Vast populations of Northern Europe were cleaved from the true Faith because the needed reforms came too late.

Saint Bernardine was one of the many bright lights of fifteenth-century Italy who did everything in his power to create a holier Church through his preaching. He was such a compelling and entertaining speaker that enormous crowds turned out to hear him, normally first thing in the morning. He encouraged devotion to the Holy Name of Jesus and often held the IHS monogram in his hand when preaching. This devotion was later incorporated as a feast day into the universal calendar of the Church. Bernardine dramatically exhorted his congregations to melt their mirrors, playing cards, perfumes, dice, wigs, and other worldly distractions in a "bonfire of the vanities" roaring near his pulpit. This was true drama.

In the Franciscan tradition, Bernardine of Siena walked everywhere. No horse or mule or carriage for the journey. He excoriated usury, superstition, and the deplorable scourge of homosexual acts, in the starkest terms. Compared to the modern penchant for market research, polling, and tailoring a message to audience expectations, Saint Bernardine was fearless. He spoke the unvarnished truths of his religion to the adherents of the same. Preaching, he understood, was an essential charism of the Priesthood of Christ, not an add-on. Saint Bernardine also published, far ahead of his time, works on entrepreneurship, business practices, a just wage, and the determining of just values for a product or service. Saint Bernardine was a sophisticated thinker with a common touch.

The fact that Saint Bernardine lived almost into the age of the printed book meant that many of his sermons were accurately preserved. It also meant that images of his likeness were uniform and accurate. A famous painting by El Greco shows the emaciated friar in a worn Franciscan habit, the three knots on his white cincture visible, representing poverty, chastity, and obedience. His right hand holds a standard bearing the monogram of the name of Jesus—IHS. In his left hand is a book, perhaps the Bible. And at his feet are three bishops' miters. Saint Bernardine was three times offered to be made a bishop and three times he said, "No." Thus, in addition to all of his other considerable virtues, our saint also possessed the queen of the virtues — humility. Bernardine of Siena was the Saint Paul of his era and was canonized in 1450, just six years after he died, numerous miracles having already been attributed to his intercession.

Saint Bernardine of Siena, inspire all preachers to not count the personal cost of stating uncomfortable truths but instead to suffer the repercussions of honest talk. Help priests to fortify their preaching with impeccable lives of prayer, fasting, devotion, and virtue, just as you did.

May 21: Saint Christopher Magallanes, Priest and Martyr, and Companions, Martyrs

Fr. Magallanes: 1869–1927; 22 priests and 3 laymen: 1915-1937, the majority killed between 1926-1929
Optional Memorial; Liturgical Color: Red

A Mexican bloodletting

The governor of Mexico's Tabasco state in the 1920s, Garrido Canabal, was so insanely anti-Catholic that he named his three sons Lenin, Satan, and Lucifer. He was also a farmer and named one of his bulls "God," a hog "Pope," a cow "Mary," and a donkey "Christ." He ordered the removal and destruction of all crucifixes from public buildings and graveyards in Tabasco. Painful photographs of the destruction prove that it happened. For his vicious persecution of the Church, he was elevated to a national cabinet position in the 1930s. Canabal was a political protégé of the Mexican president, and later strongman, Plutarco Calles. Calles was an illegitimate child, born to unmarried parents. Calles hated being called an illegitimate child and especially resented the Roman Catholic Church for this title of illegitimacy. In time, Calles became a devout believer in the religion of atheism, eagerly shared his beliefs with others, and put great energy into evangelizing others to his side. As governor of the state of Sonora, he expelled all Catholic priests. As president of Mexico, he carried out an overtly violent, ferocious, scorched-earth attack on Catholicism without par in the twentieth century. Priests were killed for no other reason than for being priests. This led to a popular counterreaction known as the Cristero War, a slow burn of assassinations, pitched battles, skirmishes, and reprisals. Central Mexico was in a full-blown meltdown in the 1920s.

For a visitor to Mexico today, or to anyone familiar with its culture, such events are difficult to imagine or comprehend. Mexico harbors one of the most vibrant Catholic cultures in the entire world, thick with devotions, processions, Masses, feast day celebrations, and religious song and dress. Yet the Cristero War did happen, and not a thousand years ago.

The militant, anti-religious mentality of Anglo-Saxon secular humanism is familiar to many believers today. It is the air we breath. This educated secularism opposes the very idea of God, exalts a narrow understanding of freedom, denigrates the concept of belief, and transposes science as an object of faith rather than a formal creed. The militant anti-religious mentality of 1920s Mexico, and of other culturally Catholic nations, was and is different from Anglo-Saxon secularism. Anti-Catholicism in Catholic nations expresses itself in anticlericalism. Hatred is unleashed against bishops and priests and their instruments of ministry—altars, crucifixes, vestments, rosaries, statues, etc.—not so much against creeds or ideas. You don't need to read Nietzsche or to master the Enlightenment canon to hate the Church. Whereas Anglo Saxon secularism wages its battles in the higher echelons of university classrooms and the courts, Latino anticlericalism is not too

MAY

Wall of Martyrs, San Pedro Tlaquepaque, Jalisco, Mexico

complex. Just kidnap a priest, blindfold him, tie his hands tightly behind his back, and shoot him in the head. Anticlericalism liquidates its enemies against the dirty brick wall behind the local police station. No courtrooms are needed.

Today's saint, and the others canonized with him, were caught in the storm that was Plutarco Calles. Father Magallanes was a priest of humble origins similar to those of Calles, but Magallanes walked a different path than the strongman. After working the land as a youth for his poor family, he entered the seminary and was ordained a priest in 1899. He then served faithfully as a chaplain and as a pastor to the Huichole Indians for many years. By middle age, he was a priest of some stature. But the otherwise ordinary arc of his life took an extraordinary turn when, on May 21, 1927, he was on his way to celebrate the Feast of St. Rita of Cascia (May 22) in a small village. A shootout between Cristeros and Federal forces near the village led to Father Magallanes' arrest, along with a brother priest, Father Caloca. There were no accusations and no trial. There was neither the presentation of evidence nor the right of defense, since priests had no civil rights in Mexico at the time. On May 25, 1927, the two priests were led to the courtyard of a municipal building for what always happened next. Father Magallanes stated: "I am innocent and die innocent. I absolve with all my heart those who seek my death and ask God that my blood bring peace to a divided Mexico." The priests absolved each other, spoke some few words of comfort, and then were shot to death by a firing squad of fellow Mexicans in soldiers' uniforms. Father Caloca's last words were: "For God we lived and for Him we die."

Twenty-five martyrs are commemorated today. All were diocesan priests, except for three laymen who died with their parish priest. They died in eight different Mexican states under circumstances similar to those of Frs. Magallanes and Caloca. One was hung from a mango tree in a town square, another from an oak in the country; one was shot for not revealing the confessions of his co-prisoners, one was bayoneted and beaten to death; one was shot and his body placed on railroad tracks to be mutilated by a train. The executioner of one priest refused to fire his rifle. He was shot right after the priest. Pope Saint John Paul II beatified the group in 1992 and canonized them in 2000. In addition to Frs. Magallanes (Cristóbal

Magallanes Jara) and Caloca (Agustín Caloca Cortés), these martyrs were: Román Adame Rosales, Rodrigo Aguilar Alemán, Julio Álvarez Mendoza, Luis Batis Sáinz, Mateo Correa Magallanes, Atilano Cruz Alvarado, Miguel De La Mora, Pedro Esqueda Ramírez, Margarito Flores Garcia, José Isabel Flores Varela, David Galván Bermúdez, Salvador Lara Puente (layman), Pedro de Jesús Maldonado Lucero, Jesús Méndez Montoya, Manuel Morales (layman), Justino Orona Madrigal, Sabás Reyes Salazar, José María Robles Hurtado, David Roldán Lara (layman),Toribio Romo González, Jenaro Sánchez Delgadillo, David Uribe Velasco, and Tranquilino Ubiarco Robles.

Father Magallanes, your quiet witness and noble death are an inspiration to all who suffer physical violence for the faith in unknown ways and in unknown places. May your intercession and courage be an inspiration for all priests, laymen, and religious who are tempted to bend in the winds of persecution.

May 22: Saint Rita of Cascia, Religious
c. 1386–1457
Optional Memorial; Liturgical Color: White
Patron Saint of abuse victims, sterility, and difficult marriages

She suffered for two spouses

Rita Lotti gave birth to her first son at the age of twelve. Fortunately the child was not born out of wedlock. Rita's husband had been chosen for her by her parents, and they married when she was twelve. Throughout eighteen years of marriage, Rita endured her husband's insults, physical abuse, and infidelity until the loathful man was stabbed to death by one of his many enemies. Rita pardoned her husband's killers and impeded her two sons from avenging their father's death. Marriage ends with death, so Rita was free after her husband's passing to satisfy a holy desire of her youth and entered an Augustinian convent. The leadership of the local Augustinians was reluctant to admit Rita, however, because she was not a virgin. Despite wide precedence for widows entering religious life, Rita was compelled to wait a number of years before receiving the habit.

Rita was a model nun who lived to the fullest the spiritual requirements of her age. She was obedient, generously served the sick of the convent, and shared her wisdom of human nature, especially regarding marital distress, with the lay women who sought her out. Sister Rita was also devoted to prayer and meditated so deeply on the Passion of our Lord that she experienced a ministigmata. Instead of open wounds in her hands oozing blood, as Saint Francis and Saint Padre Pio displayed, a small wound appeared on Rita's forehead. It was as if a thorn from Christ's crown had penetrated the tightly wrapped flesh on her skull. There was no thorn visible, of course, just as no nails or spears pierced the bodies of other stigmatists. Rita's wound refused to heal for a number of years. The unique statue, or image, showing a nun with a thorn stuck in her forehead is Saint Rita, making her one of the most easily identifiable people on the calendar of Catholic saints.

After Saint Rita died of natural causes, her body did not deteriorate. She was placed in an ornate tomb, her extraordinary holiness was attested to in writing, and healing miracles were petitioned for and soon granted through her intercession. These many cures led to Rita's beatification in 1626 and her canonization in 1900. Leathery black skin still covers Saint Rita's habited body as she peacefully reposes in a glass coffin in her shrine in Cascia, Italy. She is invoked as a kind of female Saint Jude, a patroness of impossible causes, particularly those related to the difficult vocation of marriage.

Saint Rita was both a physical and a spiritual mother. She was a spouse of Christ—a perfect man, and of her husband—a flawed man. She knew intimately the vocation both to religious and to married life, giving her a certain status, or credibility, with both consecrated and married women, which few others saints enjoy. Rita's dual vocation has given her a dual attraction, which is likely the cause of her fame and the continued devotion to her so many centuries after her death. In many ways, her life in the convent was not remarkable, except for the stigmata. There were surely many other nuns in Rita's era and region whose virtue and prayerfulness stood out. Yet for reasons known to God alone and which are therefore sufficient, this nun, among so many others who brimmed with holiness, is still visited in her shrine, still invoked, and still thanked for the favors that she continues to rain down from her place in heaven.

MAY

Saint Rita, through your intercession, aid all women in difficult marriages and abusive situations. Help women in distress to think rationally, to be faithful to their husbands if possible, to be devoted to their vows if they are able, and yet to flee if they are in danger.

May 25: Saint Bede the Venerable, Priest and Doctor
c. 672–735
Optional Memorial; Liturgical Color: White
Patron Saint of scholars

Life's drama is found in going deeper, not wider

There is no world bigger than a monk's cell. Those four, high walls shape thought like hard, steep banks contain the flow of a river. Rock curtains hanging on both sides force the raging river to carve a path through the landscape, always forward, always deeper. Here the tall banks stop the pounding river from pouring over into the plains. There the low banks allow the gentle current to run low and straight. A river without banks is a lake. And a mind without borders is a puddle—no forward movement and too shallow to sustain life. Borders, limits, and guardrails have expansive effects, paradoxically. A frame makes a painting burst to life; orderly lanes push traffic forward; and the edge of a canvas focuses the artist's skill. Big thoughts start with boundaries. That's why big thoughts happen in small spaces. Many thousands of monks' minds were molded by the limits of the four, cold walls of their cells. And these scholar monks and saint monks gave birth to what we now call Europe.

Today's saint was a model monk who lived his whole life in an English monastery, although he occasionally traveled to neighboring communities to teach young scholars. Venerable Bede's cell and monastery were nothing like those impressive stone structures with soaring arches and large courtyards, which still stand as icons of medieval Europe. Bede lived long, long before that golden age of monasticism. He died less than two hundred years after Saint Benedict, the founder of monasticism. The monasteries of Bede's era were more like farms, where the monks lived in a dormitory above a large chapter room or perhaps even in crude huts huddled around a squat stone church. These first simple efforts to plant religious life into English soil matured, over centuries, into a network of enormous English monasteries. And these monasteries, in their fullest flower, grew into the universities, towns, schools, hospitals, lodges, cathedrals, and trade centers of England itself, a rich garden of Catholicism known in medieval times as Mary's Dowry. Venerable Bede and his monastic brothers planted. Later generations harvested. And King Henry VIII then confiscated the garden and handed it over to his friends, who uprooted its most beautiful plants. Ironically and sadly, the tombs of many English saints, including Venerable Bede, lie today in Protestant churches.

From his cell in remote England, Bede was enmeshed in the Church matters of his day. He was involved in the long simmering dispute over the date of Easter, promoted the practice of using Christ's birth as the starting date for calendars, translated Christian works from Latin or Greek into Anglo-Saxon (to the immense good of the growth of the Church in England), and authored numerous works, the most famous of which is a history of the Church in England until his days. He was, in short, a prolific and wide-ranging scholar. In 1899, Pope Leo XIII honored that reputation by naming him a Doctor of the Church, the only native of England to be so honored.

Thomas à Kempis, in his classic *The Imitation of Christ*, writes that every time a monk leaves his cell he comes back less a man. In his cell the monk learns everything he needs to know about himself, the world, and God. It is *inside* of our vocations that we find God's will and our own fulfillment. A deep and abiding commitment to a specific person, religion, home, job, school, parish, spouse, and family is the stuff of life. Wandering is fun for a while. Commitment, though, is more exciting in the long run. The banks of the river must be built up. The edges and borders stacked high. The rails set in place. Then, and only then, life starts to be lived. To go deeper, not wider. To run those roots down deep into the moist soil. When we leave the four corners of our commitments and vocation, it may be liberating for a while, but time rectifies the deception. Our vocation is our home, and in that home we find happiness, make others happy, and satisfy the divine plan of the God who made us.

Bede the Venerable, we see in your life a model of commitment to one place, one idea, one love, and one Church. We ask your intercession to aid all scholars, all monks, and all who waver, to stay at their desk, their kneeler, or their work bench to fulfill the task at hand.

MAY

May 25: Saint Gregory VII, Pope, Religious
c. 1015–1085
Optional Memorial; Liturgical Color: White

A pope dies on the run

The last words spoken by Pope Saint Gregory VII were "I have loved justice and hated iniquity, that is why I die in exile." His enemies would have claimed that they loved justice equally as much but understood it differently, which is why the pope had to die on the run. No one really wins epic battles for power, though one side may prevail in the short run. Everyone loses something in a fight: some their dignity, others their property, their position, or maybe their teeth. There is no such thing as a win-win outcome. Pope Gregory VII was a scrappy fighter who boxed his powerful opponents for years. Yet he didn't fight for his own honor, wealth, or position, but because he believed that "the blessed Peter is father of all Christians, their chief shepherd under Christ, (and) that the holy Roman Church is the mother and mistress of all the churches." He battled for the right of the Bishop of Rome to govern the Church's internal life free of interference from worldly powers. Pope Gregory's victories and losses colored all of medieval history and established key precedents for the perennial tensions between Church and State which continue until today.

Gregory VII was baptized as Hildebrand in the Tuscany region of Italy. He received an excellent education from Roman tutors, including one who later became Pope Gregory VI. Most of his adult life was dedicated to serving various popes in important diplomatic and administrative roles. He was one of the most essential papal advisers of his era, even helping to craft the Church law limiting papal conclaves to cardinals alone. While still a deacon, Cardinal Hildebrand was chosen Pope in 1073 by popular acclamation. He refused to be seated on the papal throne as the result of such an outlaw election and went into hiding. Not until a proper vote of the cardinals took place did Hildebrand accept his election as canonically legitimate. He was shortly thereafter ordained a priest and bishop and then crowned Pope Gregory VII on the Feast of the Chair of Saint Peter, June 29, 1073.

MAY

When Pope Gregory VII first sat on the throne of Saint Peter and gazed out at the universal church, he did not peer through rose-colored glasses. Long firsthand experience of the world made him no novice, so he set about with great determination to implement needed reforms. His twelve-year papacy would be one of the most consequential in history. Gregory first sought to carve out a space for the papacy to operate free from German meddling in its internal affairs. It was common at the time for princes, kings, and other powerful laymen to appoint clerics to their positions and to "invest," or clothe, new bishops at their Ordination Masses with the symbols of office, such as their pastoral staff, miter, and ring. Gregory decreed an end to this practice, not least because of the confusion it engendered about who was the source of the bishop's authority. But the "lay investiture" battle would continue for centuries, leading to recriminations on all sides, including Gregory's dramatic excommunication of Emperor Henry IV and Henry's deposition—and driving into exile—of the pope. Incredibly, as late as 1903, the Holy Roman Emperor still directly intervened in a papal conclave, exercising his ancient right of veto to block a cardinal from being elected pope.

Pope Gregory VII pulled every lever at his disposal to make priestly celibacy compulsory, sought to heal the Schism of 1054 with the Orthodox, railed against simony (the purchasing of church offices), and encouraged the recovery of the holy sites in Jerusalem, a harbinger of the Crusades which commenced soon after his death. Gregory also memorialized in the clearest of terms the Church's theology of the real presence of Christ in the Holy Eucharist, a statement of faith that presaged the deep devotion to the Blessed Sacrament so characteristic of the High Middle Ages. Long before the popes were known as "Vicar of Christ," they were called "Vicar of Peter." Pope Gregory VII was a model medieval pope above personal reproach, ambitious only for the health and freedom of the Church. He represented both Christ and Saint Peter well.

Pope Saint Gregory VII, may your earthly example and heavenly intercession sustain and inspire the leaders of the Church to act impetuously, to fight ceaselessly, and to forgive generously when confronted by forces inimical to the well-being of the Church.

May 25: Saint Mary Magdalene de' Pazzi, Virgin
1566-1607
Optional Memorial; Liturgical Color: White
Patron Saint of the sick

Life's true drama is on the inside

Today's Carmelite saint was the Italian counterpart to Spain's famous Carmelite, Teresa of Ávila, although Mary Magdalene de' Pazzi is less well known than her Spanish contemporary. Teresa was a well-traveled and extroverted reformer and founder of a large and vital branch of the Carmelite Order. Mary Magdalene, on the other other hand, was not even a Mother Superior, much less a founder, and followed the ancient observance of Carmel, not its "Teresian," or discalced, offshoot.

Named Caterina at her baptism, today's saint was from a wealthy, pious, and respected Florentine family who expected their only daughter to marry young and marry well. But young Caterina was well trained in the things of God from the start and destined for a higher calling. While Caterina was still a girl, her spiritual director taught her the benefit and discipline of meditating half an hour a day. At the tender age of twelve, she experienced her first ecstasy. She gazed transfixed at the gorgeous sun setting over the rolling countryside and shook at the awesome beauty of God's creation. Her mother was there, but little Caterina was speechless, unable to describe what hidden forces caused her body to tremble so.

When she was sixteen, she entered a Carmelite convent, over her family's initial objections. Taking the religious name of Mary Magdalene, she experienced a number of shocking spiritual events, which were documented and witnessed by her fellow Carmelites and by priest confessors. The young nun was rapt in God for weeks and months on end. She shook violently and showed signs of the stigmata. In her ecstasies, she received a crown of thorns from Jesus to share in His sufferings and a ring to symbolize her mystical marriage to Him. She lived on only bread and water for years, in reparation for the sins of mankind. When a priest ordered her to eat the simple fare of the convent, she became ill and had to return to her more meager nourishment. After one ecstatic vision, a near-death experience, Mary Magdalene described how she had given her

MAY

St. Mary Magdalene de' Pazzi

heart to Jesus and how He had returned it to her with the purity of the Virgin Mary's own heart. Jesus Christ had even hidden Saint Mary Magdalene in His side, subjugating her will and desires to His own.

These many years of intense fireworks in her soul were followed by dark years of dryness and isolation. She felt a painful separation from Jesus her Spouse. During this time, Saint Mary Magdalene struggled with prideful self-love, distaste for God, and the all too common temptations of the flesh and the devil. But she persevered and became novice mistress of the Carmel, recommending poverty, obedience, and abandonment to the will of God as the surest forms of holiness. Mary Magdalene died young, exhausted from her spiritual contests, fasts, and demanding life of prayer. Behind her spectacular displays of spirituality was the day in and day out austerity of Carmelite convent life: the longing for a nice piece of meat, going to bed on an empty stomach, knees and hips aching from scrubbing the floor for endless hours, no dessert to satisfy the sweet tooth, kneeling before the Blessed Sacrament and almost falling forward due to eyes burning with lack of sleep. Only by long practice do actions mature into habits and habits into the highest virtues. The proving ground of a strict convent proves a soul, and only then might spiritual flowers bloom. Only then might bright ecstasies sparkle against the dark curtain of night, to the wonder and awe of all around.

For Mary Magdalene, Christ was not all rod and lash. She was a happy nun who played her part in keeping her convent running. She kept her personality, like all stigmatists and elite spiritual warriors, yet became one with Christ in a mysterious manner best described in poetic rather than theological terms. Her renown was widespread and her cult immediate. She was canonized in 1669. Her body lies in peace in her native Florence and is still incorrupt.

Saint Mary Magdalene de' Pazzi, we ask your divine intercession before your Mystical Spouse to give all Religious the gift of perseverance, obedience, and poverty. Your spiritual ecstasies were unique—and destined for few. Grant those gifts that are common—and destined for many.

May 26: Saint Philip Neri, Priest
1515–1595
Memorial; Liturgical Color: White
Patron Saint of Rome, humor and joy

Everyone saw the halo

Saint Philip Neri often begged alms from his wealthy friends and acquaintances to redistribute to needy children. On one occasion, he approached a friend, held out his hand, and asked him, once again, for a few coins: "How about some help for the children." The man slapped him hard across the face. Saint Philip quickly recovered from the shock, extended his cupped hand again, and said, "That was for me, now how about something for the children?"

Saint Philip was born into a well-educated, Catholic, middle-class home. He carried himself all his life with the bearing of an amiable, well-read, finely dressed, shrewd individual who knew no enemies. After growing up in Florence, he moved to Rome and spent many years as a layman studying theology and helping the poor in practical ways. While still a layman, Philip founded a group to care for the many impoverished pilgrims who came to Rome. He befriended the great reformer Saint Ignatius of Loyola, who wanted Philip to become a Jesuit. But after encouragement from his confessor, Philip was ordained a secular priest in 1551. Soon afterward, he had to formalize the large following he generated that wanted to live more fully the life he preached and modeled.

MAY

Saint Philip was so well loved and so well known in Rome that he is sometimes called its "Third Apostle" after Saints Peter and Paul. His personality radiated a natural warmth and cordiality. His priestly ministry could be fairly characterized as "evangelization by walking around." He walked the streets of Rome from end to end continually throughout his long life. His life was a long conversation with a thousand characters on street corners, in shops, factories, churches, parks—wherever. He reached out to the destitute, prostitutes, poor children, and the uneducated. Saint Philip would often gather a group to visit seven churches in a row. As they went from one church to another, the group would picnic and listen to the musicians whom Saint Philip brought along for entertainment. These outings, understandably, became hugely popular.

Leaders, intellectuals, musicians, and scholars were also drawn to him, in addition to common folk, and formed the impressive circle of committed Catholics who first joined his apostolic efforts. Saint Philip and his companions were given charge of a parish where they held evening sessions filled with song, readings from the lives of the martyrs, the praying of the psalms, and rich conversation. Saint Philip called these gatherings the "oratory," in part because the participants also listened to musical pieces called "oratorios." So when it came time to formalize his newly founded community in Church law, the name "Oratory" was chosen. The Congregation of the Oratory, which is still thriving today, was recognized by the Holy Father in 1575 and given the magnificent, new parish of Santa Maria in Varicella, known as Chiesa Nuova (The New Church), in the heart of Rome. Oratorians are mostly diocesan priests and some laymen who live together in a loose brotherhood, taking no vows, while pursuing various individual ministries. The many dozens of oratories around the world are joined in an informal confederation, whereas canonical bonds tie the many houses of a religious order together in a far tighter union.

Saint Philip is one of the bright lights of the Counter-Reformation. He blazed a new path, like other reformers. But the new path he blazed was really just the old path, walked differently. Saint Philip was the silent observer, the cheerful listener, the priest always there, who spoke hard truths but always bent on the non-essentials. He mortified himself but never talked about it. He was poor but wore nice clothes. He looked like everyone else, yet…there was that intangible something: the sparkle in his eye, his polish, his lively concern, his clever wit, his courtesy, his wide education, his humor, and his constant turning of the conversation back to God. He was like everyone else, but he wasn't, really. He radiated what twentieth-century psychologists would call the "halo effect." Everyone saw the invisible halo casting a glow over Saint Philip, and people crowded around to stand in his mellow light.

Saint Philip did not start a university, reform an institution, write a classic, or formulate a new rule. He changed the world the only way it can truly be changed—one soul at a time. This army of one was canonized in 1622. His body rests in a glass coffin in Chiesa Nuova, the sumptuous Mother Church of the Oratory, where pilgrims come in faith, kneel before him, and seek his powerful intercession.

Saint Philip Neri, your good nature and charm, united with your theological orthodoxy and life of deep prayer, made you a powerful apostle for the people of Rome. May all evangelists, especially priests, see in your openness to others a pathway of changing the world.

May 27: Saint Augustine of Canterbury, Bishop
Early Sixth Century–604
Optional Memorial; Liturgical Color: White
Patron Saint of England

The Church's Augustus conquered by example

Gaius Octavius Thurinus was a noble Roman. Julius Caesar became his stepfather when he adopted Octavius, posthumously, in his will. Octavius then added his dead stepfather's name to his own, becoming Gaius Julius Caesar Octavianus. He defeated his political enemies in 31 B.C. and thus became the first Emperor of Rome. To recognize his status, the Roman Senate added another link to his long chain of names—Augustus. And it is as Augustus that he is known to history. This very Augustus called for the census forcing Mary and Joseph to transfer to Bethlehem: "In those days a decree went out from Emperor Augustus that all the world should be registered" (Lk 2:1). Augustus reigned well and lived long, until 14 A.D. He is considered the iconic Emperor of the "Pax Romana," a tranquil, vast, expanding, organized, rich, united, and unconquerable realm, an enormous map of which Augustus pondered from his throne in Rome. The eighth month was renamed to honor Augustus during his own lifetime.

But greatness is not limited to the Roman Emperor or his Empire. The best of Rome was absorbed, filtered, purified, and reborn in the Catholic Church. As Rome declined, popes and bishops did not pickpocket the corpse of Rome or rifle through the drawers of its abandoned dressers. The transformation from Empire to Church was organic, slow, and unrelenting, like all true cultural change. It happened imperceptibly, year by year, person by person, family by family, town by town, until one day everything was different. The arc of cultural change doesn't have a right angle. It is fitting and poetic, then, that the Church has her own great Augustus, indirectly evoking the laurel-crowned Emperor. In fact, the Church has two Augustines: Saint Augustine of Hippo, in North Africa, a Doctor of the Church; and Saint Augustine of Canterbury, today's saint. But their marble statues are not in museums. They are in churches. Saint Augustine of Canterbury was born in an unknown year about a century after his Christian namesake's death in 430 A.D. in North Africa. He also conquered a king, like his secular namesake, but not for his own glory.

Saint Augustine of Canterbury is called the Apostle to the English (not to the British.) The history is complex. Christianity was deeply rooted in Roman Britain. British bishops attended Church Councils in France in the fourth century, and two famous Roman British Catholics well known to history lived centuries before Saint Augustine—Pelagius and Saint Patrick. But after the Romans abandoned Britain around 410 A.D., invasions of the pagan Saxons from Northern Europe mixed with native tribes to alter the cultural and religious landscape. Old Roman Britain faded as Anglo-Saxon England dawned. Christianity was relegated to the margins of the British Isles, surviving in remote regions and in an extensive network of monasteries, not parishes or dioceses, under the wise tutelage of Irish monks.

This two-hundred-year British-Irish hibernation of Catholicism was aroused from its sleep when, in 595 A.D., Pope Saint Gregory the Great had a plan. The goal? Convert King Ethelbert. Why? Because he was an Anglo-Saxon pagan. The hope? His wife was Catholic.

MAY

The means? A large missionary train. The man for the job? Saint Augustine. Our saint, an educated Benedictine monk from Rome, headed a large team that struggled through France on horseback, crossed the English Channel in simple boats, and finally walked to Ethelbert's seat of power in Canterbury. The King of all Kent heard the missionaries and…converted to Catholicism! And then all his subjects converted as well. The plan worked. Mission accomplished!

More missionaries followed. Schools were established. Monasteries were founded. Bishops were appointed. Priests were ordained. Parishes were opened. Rough Anglo-Saxon England put on the yoke of Christ and the lovely, rolling, deep green countryside of England became Mary's dowry. Nothing is known of the life of Saint Augustine before 595 A.D. He is famous because he was a missionary monk and later bishop. His life and his mission are indistinguishable. He accepted a dare from the Pope and did the impossible. He was himself the foundation stone upon which a Catholic nation built its house of faith for almost a millennium.

Saint Augustine, your long years of prayer, asceticism, and reading as a monk prepared you for greater things. May all who seek your intercession prepare themselves in times of quiet for future challenges. May all missionaries be as daring as you in fulfilling what is asked of them.

St. Augustine of Canterbury landing in Kent, England

May 29: Saint Paul VI, Pope
1897–1978
Optional Memorial; Liturgical Color: White

An erudite introvert helms the Church in stormy waters

Over the two millennia of its storied existence, the papacy has piled prestige upon power upon privilege like so many bricks in a high, impregnable, theological fortress. The Bishop of Rome is without doubt the world's greatest institutional defender of tradition. There is simply no other office which telescopes into one man all that is meant by the compressed phrase "Western Civilization." Giovanni Baptista Montini, today's saint's baptismal name, was as perfectly prepared by education and experience as any man before him to carry the torch of tradition handed to him by his predecessor Pope Saint John XXIII. Yet for all of his erudition and decades of practice walking along the high ridges of church life, the mid-1960s suddenly demanded of the Pope a mix of lace-like delicacy and raw political power alien to his sensitive character. The unity of the Church after the Council was quickly unwinding under potent centrifugal forces. In order to keep the core intact, it was no longer enough for the Pope to be just the bearer of the great tradition. Paul VI had to be Peter, a man of office and authority, yes, but also a tireless missionary like Saint Paul, and a silently courageous disciple and sign of contradiction like Saint Mary.

The future Pope Paul VI was born in the last years of the nineteenth century in Northern Italy to an educated and dignified family that was deeply committed to the Church. Giovanni was ordained a priest at the tender age of twenty-two and entered the service of the Vatican a few years later. He spent approximately thirty years serving in the central administration of the Holy See in roles placing him in close contact with three popes. He was appointed Archbishop of Milan in 1954 and a Cardinal in 1958. *"Habemus Papam"* could have been announced before the Cardinals ever mustered in the Sistine Chapel for the papal conclave of 1963, as few doubted whose experience best prepared him to be pope or who Pope Saint John XXIII wanted to succeed him. Cardinal Baptista took the name Paul, the first Pope of that name in over three hundred years. The new Pope very consciously united the stability and authority represented by Saint Peter with the zealous evangelical outreach represented by Saint Paul.

Paul VI became the first pope ever to travel to other continents, going on apostolic pilgrimages to the Holy Land, India, Colombia, the United States, Portugal, and Uganda. Paul also continued the Second Vatican Council and shepherded it to its conclusion in 1965. After the Council, Paul VI promulgated a new liturgical calendar, missal, breviary, and simplified rites for all the sacraments, thus impacting the lives of Catholics the world over in a personal way that few popes had ever done before. Paul VI was also deeply immersed in the theological and moral deliberations over the Church's response to new technologies making artificial means of contraception accessible and affordable to the masses. Paul's 1968 encyclical, *Humanae Vitae,* heroically restated the Church's perennial teaching on the immorality of using artificial means of contraception.

Although *Humana Vitae* was not as compelling and humanistic a presentation of the Church's rich teachings on married love as would later be advanced by Pope Saint John Paul II, it was replete with prophecies. Paul VI's predictions about the far-reaching and negative repercussions of the widespread use of contraceptives have all come true! No other individual or institution at the time foresaw, or anticipated in any way, even one of the ticking time bombs whose cultural shrapnel Paul inventoried with such accuracy. The intense storms that blew over *Humanae Vitae* in Northern Europe and North America lashed the aging Pope, and he never issued another encyclical. At times in the late 1960s and 1970s, it seemed as if chunks of Catholicism, Christianity's mighty rock of Gibraltar, might fall away and drop into the sea. But Paul VI's steady, if undynamic, hand avoided fissures in the Church's facade. Though no schisms surfaced during his pontificate, the Pope did publicly warn about the smoke of satan entering the temple of God.

Our saint was in many ways a tragic figure, tasked with leading a huge, complex Church in a confusing time. Paul's confessor, a holy and faithful Jesuit, said, after the Pope's death, that "if Paul VI was not a saint when he was elected Pope, he became one during his pontificate." The Church was Paul VI's perennial love and undying concern. He died on the Feast of the Transfiguration, August 6, and was buried, per his request, in a simple casket placed directly in the earth in the grottoes under St. Peter's Basilica, near so many of his predecessors who sat on the same Chair of Peter.

Pope Saint Paul VI, you resisted a swell of voices to uphold the Church's teachings on authentic human love. May all bishops and popes be as courageous as you in their fidelity to the Church's undying tradition.

May 31: Visitation of the Blessed Virgin Mary

Feast; Liturgical Color: White

Two young mothers and their treasures meet

Only in the Catholic Church would a Feast Day first celebrated in the thirteenth century be considered "new." But that is when the Visitation first appeared in some liturgical calendars. Our oldest liturgical feasts date from the apostolic period. That is, they were likely celebrated by the Apostles themselves in the years immediately following the earthly life of Christ. The original historical events of Holy Thursday, Good Friday, and Easter Sunday transformed into liturgical events so rapidly and so naturally that the earliest Christian writings are of a liturgical nature. Other Feast Days, such as Christmas, Mary the Mother of God, and the Birth of John the Baptist had to wait their turn. They are ancient but cede pride of place to the foundational events of Holy Week, just as America's Presidents' Day must cede to the more essential Independence Day. Without a country, there would no presidents, and without a death and resurrection, there would be no Christianity or Christian calendar in the first place.

The Visitation falls, liturgically, when it happened historically. Mary conceived Jesus Christ in late March. Saint John the Baptist was born in late June. And it was between these two bookends that pregnant Mary visited her pregnant cousin Elizabeth. Perhaps it was in late May. We may be surprised in heaven to discover that many of our biblically based feast days are commemorated on the exact historical dates they occurred. Would God deceive us otherwise? After all, no good father would tell the family to celebrate his son's birthday on a date other than when he was born.

MAY

It is the Gospel of Saint Luke that recounts for us so many details of Mary's life that otherwise remain untold. Saint John writes at the end of his Gospel that Jesus did and said many other things which are not written down. Perhaps the same could be said of Mary. Many words were spoken, gestures made, and events transpired, yet so much remains a mystery. Yet if we knew all there was to know about God and the things of God, then heaven would be a bore and not be heaven at all.

The Visitation is the first time that Mary publicly exercises her role as Mediator of the Son of God. God chose not only to become a man but to become such in the same way that all men do, through gestation and birth, with His virginal conception the sole miracle. Catholicism is a religion that believes in secondary causality. God directly intervenes in creation only rarely, instead inviting His creatures to perfect His raw creation by using their God-given talents. God did not cure the cancer. The skilled surgeon removed the tumor. He used the gifts God gave him. It was not a direct intervention. It was not a miracle. It was the doctor's mind and hands being put to their highest use. Mary generously mediated the Incarnation, placing her body at God's disposition. She, the Mother of the Church, carries the entire Church in her womb. She, the Ark of the Covenant, houses a treasure more precious than Moses' stone tablets of old. And she, the Morning Star, shines in the blackness before the blazing sun rises in the east, dawning a new day.

Christ's presence in Mary's womb radiates outward with x-ray power and reverberates in the words of faith which arise from Elizabeth and her child, John. Jesus' cousin leaps for joy inside his mother. And Elizabeth reacts by speaking those graceful words, which countless voices will go on to pray, in countless languages, many billions of times in the centuries since and in the ages to come: "Blessed are you among women, and Blessed is the fruit of thy womb." The Visitation is one of the sources of the Hail Mary.

Elizabeth is a prophet. We are her hearers. For a prophecy to be a prophecy, it has to become true. Elizabeth's words were true and are true. Mary is indeed blessed among women, and her fruit has indeed changed the world. Mary's humility instinctively deflects. She praises the source of all goodness, God, rather than the goodness of her own generosity. All things, save evil, can be traced back to

God. Mary is at the head of the trail in clearing the tangled path overgrown since the sin of Eve. With mankind close behind, Mary leads us back to discover anew the source of all truth, goodness, and beauty.

Mary and Elizabeth, your generosity in cooperating with God's will initiated the events of the New Testament. May we be equally generous in cooperating with God's plans for our lives, knowing the beginning but not the end, lighting a fire that warms the lives of unknown others.

JUNE

Saints are pious - piety is a virtue

JUNE

June 1: Saint Justin Martyr
c. 100–c. 165
Memorial; Liturgical Color: Red
<u>Patron Saint of philosophers</u>

The cut and thrust of philosophical debate led him to Truth

On one of his first missionary journeys, Saint Paul found himself in Syria. He was at a crossroads and needed to decide where he would travel to preach the Gospel. Do I head east and bring the Gospel to the gentiles of Mesopotamia, Persia, India, and China? Or do I travel west, to the Greeks, Romans, Franks, and the people on the rim of the Roman Sea (the Mediterranean)? The Acts of the Apostles relates the mystical event that happened next: "During the night Paul had a vision: there stood a man of Macedonia pleading with him and saying, 'Come over to Macedonia and help us.' When he had seen the vision, we immediately tried to cross over to Macedonia, being convinced that God had called us to proclaim the good news to them" (Ac 16: 9–10). Macedonia is in Greece. So Saint Paul's sails opened and he tacked west. The rest is history.

In the person of Saint Paul, the Church herself turned toward Greece and her philosophical tradition. It was the plan of God that His Church would decisively encounter philosophical truth, not myth and custom, as its partner in dialogue. This intellectual engagement began the long process of melding philosophical truth with theological revelation, which transformed early, Jewish-based Christianity into something new—the powerful synthesis of theology, philosophy, spirituality, and structure known as Catholicism.

Today's saint was a philosopher in the Greek tradition, born around 100 A.D. in Samaria to Greek parents. Saint Justin wrapped himself in the white, toga-style cloak of a Greek philosopher even after his conversion. He is the most well-known apologist of the second century, the only true Christian thinker known between the time of Saint John the Evangelist and Origen in the first half of the third century. Justin mercilessly criticized the intellectual dead end of the ancient paganism in which he was raised, seeing it as not merely neutral but as an obstacle to discovering the truth.

Justin loved the idea that Christ the Logos was the same in substance but different in person from the Father. Theological truth expressed in the concepts of Greek philosophy was very satisfying to him, because it was very true. Justin also provided some of the very first words on the Holy Eucharist outside of the New Testament itself: "And this food is called among us the Eucharist...we (have) been taught that the food which is blessed by the prayer of His word, and from which our blood and flesh by transmutation are nourished, is the flesh and blood of that Jesus who was made flesh." What a clear and remarkable testament to Christianity's early belief in the Eucharist!

Justin moved to Rome to teach philosophy and spent decades there writing and interacting with the higher echelons of Roman society. But even a thoughtful intellectual was not immune from persecution for being a Christian. Sometime between 162 and 168 A.D., Justin and six companions were called to answer for their beliefs before the Prefect of Rome. The record of the trial has been preserved and shows the Prefect demanding that Justin sacrifice to the gods of Rome. Justin and his friends refuse and are threatened with torture and death. They respond: "Do as you wish; for we are Christians, and we do not sacrifice to idols." What bravado! They sternly refused to be idolaters. They were duly led away, scourged, and beheaded.

Justin chose, as the Church chose, the God of the philosophers over the false gods of paganism. This was a choice for truth over illusion. As Tertullian would later write: "Christ has said that he is truth, not custom" (De Virgin. Vel. 1, 1). The Christian God is both Father and the Prime Mover; the God of Jesus Christ and the Uncaused Causer; the God of Abraham, Isaac, and Jacob and thought thinking itself. He is Father and He is Almighty. He is everywhere, because He is nowhere. He is paternal and close at hand but forever mysterious and inaccessible. He gives a name, "I am Who am," which is a riddle. We take this complex understanding of God for granted today. But the labor of early Christians like Saint Justin Martyr dug the deep intellectual foundations into which were later driven the piers of sound doctrine. It takes very smart people to make simple points.

JUNE

Saint Justin, you surrendered your life rather than worship an idol. Your refusal to abjure your faith gives an example to all Christian intellectuals and teachers that the deepest truths are not found only on a page but must be lived, and sacrificed for, even unto death.

June 2: Saints Marcellinus and Peter, Martyrs
Mid-third Century–c. 304
Optional Memorial; Liturgical Color: Red

Their memory was preserved by their very executioner

Saint Helen went to the Holy Land and returned to Rome with remnants of the true cross of Christ. This same Helen was the mother of Constantine, the Roman Emperor who legalized Christianity in 313 and who called the Council of Nicea in 325. When Saint Helen died around 328, her Emperor-Son placed her body in a monumental, sumptuous sarcophagus of rare, porphyry marble from Egypt. The deeply carved red stone shows Roman soldiers on horseback conquering barbarians. These are not scenes likely to adorn a pious woman's tomb. It was probably meant to be Constantine's own sarcophagus, but when his mother died, he used it for her. And Constantine did one more thing for his mother. He built a large church on the outskirts of Rome over the catacombs, or burial place, of today's saints, Marcellinus and Peter, and placed his mother and her giant tomb inside of the church.

That one so famous and powerful as Constantine would build a church over the catacombs of Marcellinus and Peter, and honor this church still more with his mother's tomb, testifies to these martyrs' importance to the early Christians of Rome. And since they were martyred in approximately 304, only a decade before Constantine conquered the eternal city, their memory must still have been fresh when Christianity was legalized. Until this time, Christians worshipped in dark, hidden places. As they first stepped into the public light to build the ancient churches whose walls, pillars, and foundations are still visible today, these Christians honored those who came before them. They honored those whose deaths were all the sadder because they perished so close to the day of Christian liberation. They honored Saints Marcellinus and Peter.

JUNE

Little is known with certainty about Saint Marcellinus and Saint Peter. Tradition tells us that Marcellinus was a priest and Peter an exorcist and that they were beheaded on the outskirts of Rome. A few years after the bloody event, a little boy from Rome heard about their deaths from the mouth of their very executioner, who later became a Christian. That little boy was named Damasus, and he went on to became Pope from 366–384. Decades later, remembering the story he had heard as a child, Pope Damasus honored Marcellinus and Peter by adorning their tomb with a marble inscription recounting the details of their martyrdom as he had heard them so long ago. Unfortunately, the inscription is lost.

The circumstances of Marcellinus' and Peter's deaths were likely similar to those of other, better-documented martyrdoms: some public declaration of faith, arrest, perfunctory trial, a chance to offer sacrifice to a Roman god, a refusal, a last chance to be an idolater, a last refusal, and then a swift, businesslike beheading. It was over quickly. Then came the calm. Then came the night. And out of that darkness emerged a candle-lit procession of humble Christians, walking slowly and silently toward the place of execution. The headless corpses were placed on white sheets and carried solemnly to an underground burial niche. A small marble plaque etched with the martyrs' names was placed nearby. An oil lamp was lit and left burning. Thus the veneration began. Thus it continues today.

Marcellinus and Peter were important enough to be included in the official list of Roman martyrs and to have their names remembered in the liturgy of Rome. As the Mass celebrated in Rome became standard throughout the Catholic world, the names of Marcellinus and Peter were embedded into the Roman Canon, the First Eucharistic Prayer. And there they are read at Mass until today, more than one thousand seven hundred years after they died. The Body of Christ forgets nothing, retains everything, and purifies its memory to honor those who deserve honoring.

The catacombs and the first Basilica of Marcellinus and Peter fell into ruins at the hands of two enemies—time and the Goths. A "new" church was built nearby to replace it and is still a parish. Saint Helen's bones were removed from her imperial tomb in the twelfth century and swapped with the body of a Pope. The tomb was later emptied again and, in 1777, moved to the Vatican museums.

Hundreds of thousands of tourists walk right by the tomb every year, seeing perhaps just a huge chunk of marble, oblivious to the rich history connecting the monumental tomb to ancient Christianity and the martyrs we commemorate today.

Saints Marcellinus and Peter, help all those who seek your intercession to face persecution and intimidation of any kind, via words, or arms, or threats, with bravery and heroic resistance.

June 3: Saint Charles Lwanga and Companions, Martyrs
1860–1886
Memorial; Liturgical Color: Red
Patron Saint of African youth

Young African Christians die like the martyrs of old

Many of the faces of the saints in heaven that shine with the light of God are dark faces. North Africa was one of the first regions to be evangelized and was home to a vibrant, diverse, and orthodox Church for over six hundred years. North Africa had over four hundred bishoprics and enriched the universal Church with a wealth of theologians, martyrs, and saints. That Catholic culture drowned under the crushing waves of Arab Muslim armies that inundated North Africa in the seventh century, altering its cultural and religious landscape. Small pockets of Christianity continued to exist in isolation for a few centuries more. But by 1830, when French colonists and missionaries settled in Tunisia and Algeria, local Christianity had totally disappeared. The Christian light had gone out in North Africa centuries before.

Yet today's saints are nineteenth-century African martyrs. While North Africa has remained in the tight grip of Islam, sub-Saharan Africa has lived a contrary reality. It has embraced Christianity. Throughout the nineteenth century, daring missionary priests and religious from various European countries penetrated deep into the towns, savannas, jungles, and river deltas of the "dark continent," carrying the light of Christ. For the most part, they were well received and initiated the long and complex process of evangelization, inculturation, and education that has turned today's sub-Saharan Africa into a largely Christian region.

JUNE

ST. CHARLES LWANGA
June 3

"The infamous crime by which these young men were put to death...shows us clearly that all peoples need a moral foundation."

– *Pope Saint Paul VI*

JUNE

Charles Lwanga and his companions were all very young men, in their teens and twenties, when they were martyred. They ran afoul of their local ruler for one reason and one reason only—they were Christians and adhered to Christian morality. The ruler did not otherwise question their loyalty, devotion, or service to him. He was suspicious of the European priests who had brought the faith, wary of outside interference in his kingdom, and also eager to impress his subjects with a display of ruthlessness and power. He was also a sodomite who wanted these young men to engage in unholy sexual acts with him. For refusing to satisfy his disordered and abusive lust, they became victims of homosexual violence.

The ruler and his court questioned the young males who served as their pages and assistants to discover if they were catechumens, had been baptized, or knew how to pray. Those who answered "Yes" were killed for it. One was stabbed through the neck with a spear and another's arm was cut off before he was beheaded. But most were marched miles to an execution site, cruelly treated for a week, then wrapped in reed matts and placed over a fire until their feet were singed. They were then given one last chance to abjure their faith. None did. These tightly wrapped human candles were then thrown onto a huge pyre and reverted to the dust from whence they came. One of the executioners even killed his own son. The executioners and onlookers knew their victims had succumbed to the flames when they no longer heard them praying.

The site where these Ugandan martyrs died is now a popular shrine and a source of pride dear to the heart of African Catholics. Charles Lwanga and his companions, though new to the faith, acted with the maturity of the wise and the aged, choosing to sacrifice lives full of promise rather than surrender the pearl of greatest price—their Catholic faith.

Saint Charles Lwanga and companions, help us to be courageous in the face of threats, to stand tall for our beliefs, and to suffer ridicule and hatred rather than renounce or minimize our relationship with Christ and His truth.

JUNE

June 5: Saint Boniface, Bishop and Martyr
c. 675–754
Memorial; Liturgical Color: Red
Patron Saint of Germany

Pagans cut down a man of action in his grey hairs

In the treasury of the Cathedral of Fulda, Germany, there is a medieval Codex, a large, bound book of prayers and theological documents, which very likely belonged to Saint Boniface. The rough cover of the Codex is deeply sliced with cuts from a sword. A tradition dating back to the generations just after Saint Boniface's own time attests that he wielded this very book like a shield to ward off the blows of robbers who attacked him and a large band of missionaries in Northern Germany in 754. Our saint tried to protect himself, both metaphorically and literally, with the written truths of our faith. It was to no avail. Saint Boniface and fifty-two of his companions were slaughtered. Ransacking the baggage of the missionaries for treasure, the band of thieves found no gold vessels or silver plates but only sacred texts the unlettered men couldn't read. Thinking them worthless, they left these books on the forest floor, to be recovered later by local Christians. The Codex eventually made it into the Treasury at Fulda where it is found today. One of the earliest images of Saint Boniface, from a Sacramentary dating to 975, depicts the saint deflecting the blows of a sword with a large, thick book. The Codex is a second-class relic, giving silent witness to the final moments of a martyr.

Saint Boniface is known as the "Apostle of the Germans" and is buried in the crypt of Fulda Cathedral. However, his baptismal name was Winfrid, and he was born and raised in Anglo-Saxon England. He was from an educated family, entered a local monastery as a youth, and was ordained a priest at the age of thirty. In 716 Winfrid sailed to the continent to become a missionary to the peoples on the Baltic coast of today's Northern Germany. He was able to communicate with them because his Anglo-Saxon tongue was similar to the languages of the native Saxon and Teutonic tribes. Winfrid was among the first waves of those many Irish and Anglo-Saxon monks who saved what could be saved of Roman and Christian culture in Europe after the Roman Empire collapsed. Large migrations of Gothic peoples, mostly Arian Christians, pagans, or a confusing mix of the two, filled the vacuum created after Roman order disintegrated, and they needed to be inculcated in the faith to rebuild a superior version of the culture they had helped decimate.

Winfrid traveled to Rome the year after first arriving on the continent, where the pope renamed him Boniface and appointed him missionary Bishop of Germany. After this, he never returned to his home country. He set out to the north and proceeded to dig and lay the foundations of Europe as we know it. He organized dioceses, helped found monasteries, baptized thousands, pacified tribes, challenged tree-worshipping pagans, taught, preached, held at least one large Church Council, convinced more Anglo-Saxon monks to follow his lead, ordained priests, appointed bishops, stayed in regular contact with his superiors in Rome, and pushed the boundaries of Christianity to their northernmost limit. Boniface was indefatigable. He was in his late seventies, and still pushing to convert the unconverted, when he was surprised and slain in a remote wilderness.

Saint Boniface was well educated, and many of his letters and related correspondence survive. But he was, above all, a man of action. He was daring and fearless. He was a pathbreaker. His faith moved mountains and tossed them into the sea. His labors, combined with his great faith, are the stuff of legend. More incredibly, though, they are the stuff of truth.

Saint Boniface, through your powerful intercession, help all those who labor for the faith to be as intrepid as you were in challenging those who reject Christ. May your example of tireless witness inspire all missionaries, both at home and abroad, to persevere.

JUNE

June 6: Saint Norbert, Bishop
c. 1080–1134
Optional Memorial; Liturgical Color: White
Patron Saint of Bohemia and of expectant mothers

Thrown down like Saint Paul, he stood up a changed man

Today's saint was born into an elite Central European family with connections to imperial dynasties and the nobility of his time. He received an excellent sacred and secular education in keeping with his high status. And as a young man he received tonsure, the particular shaving of the hair on the scalp denoting one a cleric. He was then appointed a canon, a member of a bishop's inner circle who prayed the liturgical hours in common with other canons. As a young adult, Saint Norbert was well on his way to a career as an ecclesiastic typical of his era: well connected, intelligent, politically aware, committed to the Church, an adviser to princes and bishops, and materially comfortable. His life was almost indistinguishable from those of the laymen whose company he mostly kept. Norbert avoided priestly ordination and turned down a chance to become a bishop. In a one-Church world where civil power and church power were intertwined, canons lived comfortably and held a quasi-civil office which dispensed prayers, graces, and spiritual favors for which the populace paid handsomely.

If not for a near-death experience when he was thirty-five years old, Saint Norbert would be known as just Norbert, and he would be resting, forgotten, under the stone floor of a German cathedral. But one day in 1115, Norbert was riding his horse when a lightning bolt struck nearby. He was thrown hard to the ground and was unconscious for a long time but survived. It was jarring, both physically and spiritually. Norbert was changed. He was penitent. He would abandon his life of frivolity. He would take his religious commitment seriously. This powerful experience of the fleetingness of life and its pleasures compelled Norbert to deviate from the wide, crowded road he was traveling, in order to walk, instead, a narrower, stonier, less-traveled path. And as Norbert walked, he shed his past step by step until over many years Saint Norbert emerged, miter on his head, bishop's crozier in one hand, and a monstrance in the other. One moment changed his life. It ceased to be just a moment, in fact, but was converted into a permanent event. God broke through, touched his deepest core, and created a new man.

Soon after this near-death experience, Norbert was ordained a priest, went on a month-long retreat, founded a monastery with his own wealth, and began to preach about the transitory nature of the world. He had the fervor of a convert, the ardor of one for whom all things were new. Life was a permanent Spring day. He sold all that he had except what was necessary to say Mass, divested himself of all his properties, and gave everything to the poor. He wore a simple habit, went barefoot, and begged for food.

St. Norbert

He started to preach throughout France and Germany and became well known. At the instigation of the Pope, he founded a religious Order, which quickly expanded. He was so well respected in Germany that, despite being the founder of an Order, he was named bishop of a large see. Saint Norbert became involved in various ecclesiastical arguments of his day of both a political and theological nature.

Saint Norbert's efforts to reform the clergy of his day were not always well received. He was spat upon and rejected. But he persevered. No one outdid him in devotion to the Holy Eucharist, which he preached about constantly. Centuries after his death his body was transferred to near Prague after the German city where he had been buried turned Lutheran. Saint Norbert is most often depicted as a bishop holding either a monstrance or a ciborium, both of which hold the Holy Eucharist. The Norbertine Order continues to thrive, nine hundred years after it was founded. Would that anyone would speak just our name nine hundred years after we die! The Church remembers her saints, preserves their memories, and ensures that the heroes of our faith are held up for emulation long after their earthly work is done.

Saint Norbert, your conversion led to your life of total dedication to Christ and the Church. This change was nourished by reception of and devotion to the Holy Eucharist. May we be continually nourished with and converted by the same food from heaven.

June 9: Saint Ephrem, Deacon and Doctor
Early Fourth Century—373
Optional Memorial; Liturgical Color: White
Patron Saint of spiritual directors

The Harp of the Holy Spirit

The Councils of Ephesus in 431 and Chalcedon in 451 ended a centuries-long scorpion dance. Bishops, theologians, and scholars from Egypt to Syria had long circled one another with suspicion, stinging their enemies with sharp words and pointed tongues. Did Jesus Christ have one or two natures? If two natures, were they joined in His will or in His person? If united in His person, at conception? Was He one person or was He two? Smart, educated men defended every shade of every subtlety of every complex question with all of their considerable skill. The answers hacked out at Ephesus and Chalcedon, whose hurly-burly political intrigues were less than inspiring, answered the relevant questions definitively, establishing orthodox teaching for all time. The theological language coined during those fifth century debates is still familiar to the Church today: *hypostatic union*, *monophysitism*, *Theotokos*, etc.

Today's saint, Ephrem, was active a century prior to the great conclusions and clarifications of the fifth-century Councils. Although Ephrem did not deviate from what later Councils would explicitly teach, he used far different language to communicate the same truths, anticipating later teachings through poetry. Saint Ephrem was a poet and a musician first and foremost. His language is more beautiful, compelling, and memorable because it is metaphorical. Exactness in words risks dryness. You can say that the average density of the air in the ship's hull eventually equaled the average density of the surrounding water. Or you can say that the ship sank like a stone to the ocean floor. You can write that a day's high dew point caused the air's water vapor content to slow evaporation. Or you can write that it was so hot and humid that people melted like candles. The Church can teach that we eat Christ's body and blood in the Holy Eucharist. Or we can speak directly to Christ with the poet Ephrem and say, "In your bread hides the Spirit who cannot be consumed; in your wine is the fire that cannot be swallowed. The Spirit in your bread, fire in your wine: behold a wonder heard from our lips."

The Councils of Ephesus and Chalcedon taught that the one person of Jesus Christ united in Himself a fully divine nature and a fully human nature from the moment of His conception. Saint Ephrem wrote "The Lord entered (Mary) and became a servant; the Word entered her, and became silent within her; thunder entered her and his voice was still; the Shepherd of all entered her and became a Lamb…" Poetry, metaphor, paradox, images, song, and symbols. These were tools in Saint Ephrem's nimble hands. Theology for him was liturgy, music, and prayer. He was called the Harp of the Holy Spirit, the Sun of the Syrians, and the Column of the Church by his admirers, who included luminaries such as Saints Jerome and Basil.

Saint Ephrem was a deacon who declined ordination to the priesthood. He lived radical poverty, wearing a patched and dirty tunic. He had a cave for his home and a rock for his pillow. Ephrem founded a theological school and was deeply involved in catechesis through preaching, liturgy, and music. He died after contracting a disease from a patient he was caring for. Saint Ephrem is the Church's greatest Syriac language writer, proof that Christianity is not synonymous with the West or European culture. Ephrem's world thrived for centuries with its own unique Semitic identity in today's Syria, Iraq, Iran, and India. Saint Ephrem's Syria was not the "Near East," as Europeans later called the region. To him, it was just home, the deep cradle of the new way of loving God that was, and is, Christianity. Saint Ephrem was declared a Doctor of the Church by Pope Benedict XV in 1920.

Saint Ephrem, you wrote tenderly and lovingly about the truths of our faith. Help all Christian artists to stay true to the Truth and to communicate Jesus Christ to the world through beauty, music, and images that raise the mind and lift the heart to God Himself.

June 11: Saint Barnabas, Apostle
Early First Century–c. 62
Memorial; Liturgical Color: Red
Patron Saint of Cyprus

A multi-talented disciple recruits Saint Paul

Today's saint was an Apostle in the exact same sense in which St. Paul was an Apostle. Saint Barnabas was not one of the Twelve original followers of Christ nor a replacement for one of the Twelve, like Saint Matthias. But the term "The Twelve" quickly disappeared after the Gospel events, because "The Twelve" themselves propagated into dozens, hundreds, and then thousands of successor Apostles, known alternatively as *Episcopoi* or *Prebyteroi*: Overseers or Elders. Saint Barnabas is among that generation of Christian leaders whose name first surfaces immediately after the Resurrection. So although he was not in the circle of "The Twelve," he stood in the next outer ring.

The earliest name for the movement initiated by Jesus of Nazareth was "The Way." This term is used in the Acts of the Apostles and in the ancient catechetical document known as the Didache. But "The Way" was replaced early on by another term. The Acts of the Apostles explains: "Then Barnabas went to Tarsus to look for Saul, and when he had found him, he brought him to Antioch. So it was that for an entire year they met with the church and taught a great many people, and it was in Antioch that the disciples were first called 'Christians'" (Ac 11:25–26). We owe Saint Barnabas, then, the credit for the word "Christian" as the standard description of the followers of Jesus Christ.

JUNE

The persecution and martyrdom of Saint Stephen forced many Christian leaders to flee Jerusalem. The unforeseen effect of Stephen's assassination and the subsequent persecution of Christians was the spread of the Gospel into greater Syria, the Greek Islands, and North Africa. This expansion led to contact with Greek and Roman Gentiles, or non-Jews, a growth presaging the transformation of Christianity from a localized Jewish sect into a multiethnic worldwide Church. When some converts from North Africa and Cyprus went to Antioch, the capital of the Roman province of Syria, they converted a great number of Greek speakers. And when "news of this came to the ears of the church in Jerusalem...they sent Barnabas to Antioch. When he came and saw the grace of God, he rejoiced, and he exhorted them all to remain faithful to the Lord with steadfast devotion; for he was a good man, full of the Holy Spirit and of faith" (Ac 11: 22–24a).

Saint Barnabas played a crucial role in the first unfurling of the Gospel message beyond Palestine. Acting as a kind of talent scout, he lassoed Saul from his hometown of Tarsus to begin the extraordinary missionary efforts which would forever change the Church and the world. Saint Paul and Saint Barnabas are repeatedly mentioned together in the Acts of the Apostles as they traverse the port cities, the waters, and the dusty highways of the Eastern Mediterranean world. Together, they call down the Holy Spirit, commission new Apostles, confront Jews and Roman citizens alike, challenge a magician, speak to governors, and, of utmost consequence for the Church's future, convince the other Apostles not to force new converts to become Jews first and Christians later.

Saint Barnabas was a dynamic force of nature who spun like a tornado from town to town in the early Church. He was a giant of that first generation of risk-taking, manly, apostolic leaders. The citizens of Lystra in Asia Minor compared him to the Greek God Zeus. They were so impressed that they tried to crown him with garlands and to sacrifice the blood of oxen to both him and Saint Paul (Ac 14:12–18). After numerous adventures in tandem, Paul, the better preacher, writer, and organizer, ultimately sails off on his own. The last we hear of Barnabas, he is returning to the Island of Cyprus, his native land. When Saint Paul writes from his Roman prison in about 62 A.D., he mentions that Mark, the cousin of

Barnabas, is with him (Col 4:10). Barnabas' absence at Paul's side in his hour of need is a clue that Barnabas is likely dead by the year 62. Tradition tells us that Barnabas was martyred on Cyprus, perhaps by a Jewish mob angered at his successful preaching in the synagogue of Salamis. His relics and memory are particularly honored on Cyprus to this day.

Saint Barnabas, you gathered infant Christianity from its cradle and carried it into the world beyond. You poured the message of salvation into new wineskins without any guile. May all Christians be so confident, so convincing, and so successful through your intercession.

June 13: Saint Anthony of Padua
1195–1231
Memorial; Liturgical Color: White
Patron Saint of lost articles

He mastered the Word of God

Saint Anthony of Padua is a famous Franciscan saint especially honored at an impressive shrine in Padua, in Northern Italy. But he was not born as Anthony, was an Augustinian priest before he became a Franciscan, and was from Lisbon, Portugal, not Italy. Saint Anthony, along with Saint Bonaventure, another early Franciscan, lent theological heft to the somewhat esoteric movement founded by Saint Francis of Assisi. Saint Francis was uniquely sensitive and eccentric, unsuited to leadership, and vexed by the need to exercise authority. It was Saints Anthony and Bonaventure who gave the Franciscan Order credibility, who anchored it in sound theology, and who assured its survival and continued growth.

Today's saint was baptized Fernando and grew up in a privileged environment in Lisbon. He received a superior education and entered the Augustinian Order as an adolescent. While living in the city of Coimbra, he met some Franciscan brothers who had established a poor hermitage outside of the city named in honor of Saint Anthony of the Desert. Young Father Fernando was very attracted to their simple way of life. From these friars, he also heard about the martyrdom of five Franciscan brothers at the hands of Muslims in North Africa. These martyrs' bodies were ransomed and

St. Anthony and the Christ Child
Giovanni Battista Tiepolo

returned for burial in Fr. Fernando's own abbey in Coimbra. Their deaths and burials were a life-changing moment for him. The Augustinian Fr. Fernando asked, and received, permission to leave and join the Franciscans. At that point he adopted a new religious name, Anthony, from the patron saint of the hermitage where he had first come to know the Franciscan Order.

The newly christened Father Anthony then set out to emulate his martyr heroes. He sailed for North Africa to die for the faith or to ransom himself for Christians held captive by Muslims. But it was not to be. Anthony became gravely ill, and, on the return voyage, his ship was providentially blown off course to Sicily. From there he made his way to Central Italy, where his education, mastery of Scripture, compelling preaching skills, and holiness brought him deserving renown. Paradoxically, it was because Anthony received excellent training as an Augustinian that he became a great Franciscan. Saint Francis himself soon came to know Father Anthony, a man whose learning legitimized the under-educated Franciscans. Saint Francis had been skeptical of scholarship, even prohibiting his illiterate followers from learning how to read. Francis feared they would become too prideful and then abandon their radical simplicity and poverty. Saint Francis only reluctantly, several years after founding his Order, allowed some of his brothers to be ordained priests. He had originally relied exclusively on diocesan priests to minister to his non-ordained brothers, and he distrusted his followers who aspired to the honor of the Priesthood. The presence of Anthony, and later Bonaventure, changed all that.

In time, Father Anthony became a famous preacher and teacher to Franciscan communities in Northern Italy and Southern France. His knowledge of Scripture was so formidable that Pope Gregory IX titled him the "Ark of the Testament." In Anthony's Shrine in Padua, a reliquary holding his tongue and larynx recall his fame as a preacher. These organs had not disintegrated even long after the rest of his body had returned to dust. Saint Anthony is most often shown either holding the Child Jesus in his arms or holding a book, a lily, or all three. His intercession is invoked throughout the world for the recovery of lost items and for assistance in finding a spouse.

Anthony died at the age of just thirty-five in 1231, about five years after Saint Francis had died. He was canonized less than one year later. In 1946 Saint Anthony was declared a Doctor of the Church due to the richness of his sermons and writings. He was conscious as he succumbed to death. In his last moments, the brothers surrounding his bed asked him if he saw anything. Saint Anthony said simply, "I see the Lord."

Saint Anthony of Padua, we seek your powerful intercession to have the right words on our lips to inspire the faithful and to correct and guide the ignorant. Through your example, may our words also be buttressed by our powerful witness to Christ.

June 19: Saint Romuald, Abbot
951–c. 1025
Optional Memorial; Liturgical Color: White
Founder of the Camaldolese Benedictine Order

To be alone with God is not to be alone

It is easy today to slip down a technological hole into a cave piled high with televisions, video games, and the toys of virtual reality. Many technological "hermits" disappear from meaningful contact with society, and instead marinate, perpetually, in the blue glow of their screens. Retreating from sustained contact with everyday life has always been attractive for a very small number of people. These people are called monks. But a religious monk's motivation is not isolation for isolation's sake. Nor is it flight from overwhelming adult responsibilities. Today's technological monks separate themselves from society for different reasons than a religious monk does. Religious monks were not, and are not, merely recluses with antisocial or introverted personalities. They do not become monks because they are more comfortable playing war on a digital battlefield or retreating into sci-fi universes.

Although they may have an innate disposition toward the interior life, religious monks do not enter a monastery primarily to flee, or hide from, something. Instead, they run toward someone—God. A monastery is not a cave. It is an oasis. Monks seek a Christ-centered community where mortification and self-discipline are easier to practice, where a chapel and the Sacraments are always available, and where spiritual direction, Church approval, and the reinforcement of fellow monks assure the community that they are doing the will of God.

Since the time of Saint Benedict in the sixth century, there had essentially been only one monastic order in the Latin Rite Church, the Benedictines. Benedictine monasteries shone like stars in a broad constellation, blinking throughout Europe from east to west and north to south. Each monastery and school was like a vertebra strengthening the intellectual and spiritual skeleton of Europe. Over the centuries, however, and inevitably, the Benedictines atrophied, cracked from dryness, and needed new wine poured into their old wineskins. The saint who reformed Benedictine life and who founded the Cistercian Order was Saint Bernard of Clairvaux. But he was not born until 1090. It was today's saint, Romuald, much less well-known, who cleared the path for Saint Bernard and for the reform of monasticism, ensuring its survival in the middle ages.

Saint Romuald was born in the middle of the tenth century in Northern Italy. After his father killed a relative in a duel, Romuald entered a local monastery for a few weeks of penance. But the weeks turned into months and the months into years. He stayed. Unfortunately, the monks were as lukewarm as old bathwater, and Saint Romuald told them so. He had to leave. He put himself under the tutelage of a wise hermit, then traveled to Spain to live as a hermit on the grounds of a Benedictine monastery. He subsequently spent about thirty years walking the length and breadth of Italy. He had acquired a great reputation as an ascetic and master of prayer and so founded, or reformed, various monasteries which sought his assistance.

JUNE

Finally, in 1012, he settled down in Tuscany and established a reformed branch of the Benedictines. The Order was named after the man who granted Saint Romuald the beautiful land on which he first built. The donor's name was Maldolus, and the new community was thus called the Camaldolese Order. The Order still exists in several countries and continues to attract those few men and women inclined to the radical isolation, prayer, asceticism, and deep hunger for God, which only a hermit's life can satisfy.

Saint Romuald planted the seed of his Order in the Benedictine garden. But Camaldolese monks emphasize solitude more than their monastic cousins. In a typical Benedictine monastery, every single monk places his oar in the water to pull the monastery's school, or orchard, or farm, forward. The Camaldolese tradition is more hermit based (eremitical) while allowing some community based (cenobitical) life. Camaldolese monks generally live in individual structures but pray the Mass and Liturgy of the Hours together daily in the Church. They live simplicity, penance, and contemplation more intensely due to their total focus on these goals to the exclusion of all outside apostolates. Unlike modernity's reclusive technological monks enraptured by their screens, the Camaldolese choose to live without phones, the internet, or television. The tabernacle is their screen, and the scene stays the same. With this intense focus on solitude and prayer, Camaldolese monks perpetuate, in their narrow, unique, and faithful way, the vision of their pioneering founder.

Saint Romuald, by your intense example of prayer, penance, and solitude, assist all the faithful to put God above all things, to conquer themselves before any other mountain, and so come to know themselves, and their Maker, more deeply.

JUNE

June 21: Saint Aloysius Gonzaga, Religious
1568–1591
Memorial; Liturgical Color: White
Patron Saint of Catholic youth and plague victims

Though he had many possessions, he did not go away sad

The Jesuit Order, from its very founding, had a sharp sense of its educational superiority, its fidelity to the Holy Father, and its mission to educate and spiritually guide the elites among the courts and aristocracies of Europe. The Order did not, however, develop a strong community identity. There were, and are, common houses. But Jesuit communities built on common prayer, meals, and apostolates were rare. Much more common was the Jesuit alone, trekking under the canopy of a Canadian forest, riding the waves like a cork in a boat off the coast of India, or hiking the narrow mountain pathways in the mists of the high Andes. Where there was one Jesuit, there were all Jesuits. Each man embodied his entire Order. It was a community of many ones. Jesuits were united by their vows, their long education, and their common mission. Actually living, praying, eating, relaxing, and working together, so crucial to the common life of other Orders, did not play an equivalent role among the Jesuits.

Jesuit superiors were aware of the dangers that isolation might pose to unity. So they encouraged, and even mandated, a means to sew into one fabric the patches of a thousand lives being lived across the globe. Letters! Jesuits were required to write letters to their superiors, giving regular accounts of their work. These letters had to be detailed, instructive, and inspiring. After they were reviewed, the most edifying were published and distributed to Jesuit houses. Through these letters, the Order was made one. Every Jesuit knew what at least some of his brothers were doing for God and the Church. These collections of letters, known as the Jesuit Relations, were eventually distributed beyond the confines of the Order. By the seventeenth and eighteenth centuries, the Relations were often exciting best sellers recounting the apostolic exploits of isolated Jesuits walking along the rim of Christendom.

It was just such an inspiring letter, or relation, from India that inspired today's saint, Aloysius Gonzaga, to become a Jesuit. Saint

ST. ALOYSIUS GONZAGA
June 21

"I knew the Blessed Aloysius to be a person of great humility. He despised himself, yielded to all, and sought every opportunity of lessening himself in the esteem of others. He was given to extraordinary mortification, was very devout, spending much time in prayer and in union with our Lord God..."

– *A professor's testimony in St. Aloysius' canonization process*

Aloysius was known to his family as Luigi, Aloysius being the Latinized version of his baptismal name. He was the eldest of seven children born into an aristocratic family from Northern Italy. Kings and Queens and Cardinals and Princes ate at the family table, were family themselves, or were at least friends or acquaintances. Young Luigi knew, and detested, the frivolous existence lived by so many in his aristocratic milieux. He also suffered from various physical infirmities, which produced that vulnerability and perspective which leads so clearly and directly to a deep dependence on God.

After receiving his First Communion at about the age of twelve, he came to personally know the great future saint Cardinal Charles Borromeo, who would later be his confessor and spiritual director. Borromeo was a Jesuit. His example, together with Aloysius' reading about the works of Jesuit missionaries, convinced him to enter the Jesuit Novitiate, against his family's wishes. So Aloysius went to Rome to begin his studies. And there he grew to embrace those of lesser education and refinement than himself. He volunteered to work bringing victims of a plague to a Jesuit hospital, despite his personal revulsion at the patients' decrepit physical conditions. After his own physical limitations restricted his participation in this corporal work of mercy, he still persevered and insisted on returning to the hospital over his superiors' objections.

While working in the hospital, Aloysius contracted the plague from a patient he personally cared for, was incapacitated shortly thereafter, and, a few months later, died on June 21, 1591. He was twenty-three. His reputation for purity, prayerfulness, and suffering led many to consider him a saint soon after his death. Aloysius was beatified just fourteen years later, in 1605, and canonized in 1726. He is buried in the Church of Saint Ignatius of Loyola in Rome. His contribution to the Jesuit canon was not a pagan tribe converted, a new ocean crossed, or an unknown language catalogued. His letter was his life, and it was to die young and to die holy.

Saint Aloysius, you laid all your treasures, including your youth, on an altar to God. May your example of generosity, and your service to the sick and dying, inspire all Catholic youth to give God the gold of their early years, not just the silver of middle age or the bronze of their retirement.

JUNE

June 22: Saint Paulinus of Nola, Bishop
c. 354–431
Optional Memorial; Liturgical Color: White
Patron Saint of bell makers

The best of Rome—the best of the Church

Saint Paulinus was to the manor born. And it was a very nice manor. He was raised on an aristocratic estate near Bordeaux, France, in an elite Roman family replete with senators and other high officials of empire. Paulinus received a superior education from a well-known tutor and served, while still in his twenties, as Consul of Rome and Governor of Campania in Southern Italy. He was humble, sage, gentle, well read, and intellectually curious. Paulinus represented, in short, the very best of Rome. He would, in time, represent the very best of the Church.

While serving as Governor of Campania, Paulinus witnessed the simple but sincere piety of the common people who went on pilgrimage to the shrine of Saint Felix of Nola, who had suffered for the faith around 250 A.D. The people's faith moved Paulinus to his core and planted a seed in the soil of his soul. Paulinus suffered personal setbacks due to the political machinations inherent to empires, which awakened him to the fleeting nature of power and prestige. He moved to Milan and studied in the school of Saint Ambrose. When Paulinus returned to Bordeaux, he was baptized by the Bishop. The seed of faith planted in Campania had germinated in Milan and flowered in Bordeaux. It would bear fruit for decades to come.

Paulinus married a holy Christian woman from Barcelona, and the two soon became three. But their son died after only a few days. Paulinus and his wife were thunderstruck. Another turning point. Face to face with the mystery of suffering in its crudest form, they threw their lives at God's feet. They abandoned their considerable material wealth and began to lead lives of continual prayer and asceticism. Paulinus rightly noted that poverty was not the goal, but the means to a closer bond with Christ: "...the athlete does not win because he strips himself, for he undresses precisely in order to begin the contest, whereas he only deserves to be crowned as victorious when he has fought properly."

JUNE

Paulinus, though married, was ordained a priest around 394 and then returned to the land that had first nourished his faith—Nola, in Compania. He would never leave it. After his wife's death around 410, Paulinus received episcopal ordination and served as Bishop of Nola until his death. He was part of a broader tradition of educated Roman men of the fourth and fifth centuries who served the Church as bishops rather than the empire as governors. As Bishop, Paulinus' greatness revealed itself. Although he never wrote theological or scholarly works like Saint Jerome, he maintained a steady correspondence with this great biblical scholar and many others, including Saint Martin of Tours. Paulinus wrote to a North African bishop whose close friend had just had a powerful conversion. Paulinus was curious and asked the bishop for more information. The friend's name was Augustine, and his response to Paulinus was the "Confessions." History has Paulinus of Nola to thank for the world's first autobiography, the groundbreaking work of the great Saint Augustine. Paulinus and Augustine became close friends, although they probably never met. Saint Augustine even wrote: "Go to Campania...there study Paulinus, that choice servant of God." If a man is known by the caliber of his friends, Paulinus' many impressive friends speak powerfully to his sterling character.

Saint Paulinus was a master of the art of friendship, particularly spiritual friendship. He understood the Church, the Body of Christ, as a forum where true friendship flourishes. He wrote to Saint Augustine: "It is not surprising if, despite being far apart, we are present to each other and, without being acquainted, know each other, because we are members of one body, we have one head, we are steeped in one grace, we live on one loaf, we walk on one road and we dwell in the same house." Beautiful! The Church is a communion of souls, a theological and sacramental family where deeper relationships take root and flower. Saint Paulinus is still venerated in Nola and its environs, where on his Feast Day the faithful carry in procession enormous lily-adorned towers in which stand large statues of Saint Paulinus.

Saint Paulinus of Nola, may your humility, education, and serenity be an example to all who are searching for God. May they imitate you in finding Him, in loving Him, and in dedicating their lives to Him amidst a large circle of like-minded friends.

June 22: Saints John Fisher, Bishop and Martyr, & Thomas More, Martyr

John Fisher: 1469–1535; Thomas More: 1478–1535
Optional Memorial; Liturgical Color: Red
Patron Saint of the Diocese of Rochester (Fisher)
and of lawyers and politicians (More)

They would not bend to the marriage

In 1526 a German painter named Hans Holbein could not find work in Basel, Switzerland. The Reformation had come to town. It shattered the stained glass, burned the wooden statues, and sliced up the oil paintings. Protestants don't "do" great art. There were no more commissions. So Holbein went north, to Catholic England, in search of wealthy patrons for his craft. On his way, he passed through the Netherlands to procure letters of introduction from the great humanist Desiderius Erasmus. Erasmus was a friend of Sir Thomas More, an English humanist of the highest caliber. And thus it came to pass that one fine day, in England in 1527, Thomas More sat patiently while Holbein's brush worked its magic.

Holbein's extraordinary portrait of Thomas More captures the man for all seasons, as one contemporary called More, at the pinnacle of his powers. More's head and torso fill the frame. There is no need for context, landscape, or a complex backdrop. More's mind is what matters. He is what matters. Nothing else. The shimmering velvet of his robes, the weighty gold chain of office resting on his shoulders, the detailed rose badge of the House of Tudor lying on his chest, all tell the viewer something important—this is not a frivolous man. He serves the King. His work is consequential. He also wears a ring. He is married and has children. He dons a cap. It is England, and he is cold. His stubble is visible. He is tired from overwork and did not have time to shave. He holds a small slip of paper—perhaps a bribe he rejected. His gaze, slightly off center, is earnest, serious, and calm. It is almost as if he is searching the room, attentive to any threat lurking behind the painter. He is watchful. The entirety of the work conveys that elusive quality that denotes great art—interior movement. The gears of More's brain are rotating. His personality has force. The viewer feels it.

JUNE

Saint Thomas More was the greatest Englishman of his generation. In a land with a highly educated aristocratic class, his erudition was unequalled. He was a devoted family man who carried out an extensive correspondence with his children and ensured that his daughters were as well educated as his sons. He served the English crown faithfully both at home and abroad. He charmed his many friends with a rich and engaging personality. He published scholarly works and communicated with other humanists of his era. Yet despite all of these accomplishments, the fraught times he lived in eventually overwhelmed him. He could not save his own head.

More was a thoughtful and serious Catholic. He refused to bend to the will of King Henry VIII regarding divorce and Henry's self-appointment as head of the Church in England. For his silence, or lack of explicit support for Henry, More was brought to court, where a perjurer's words knifed him in the heart. More was condemned to death by beheading. This was a favor from the King, who admired More but could not brook his dissent. More had originally been sentenced to a far crueler form of capital punishment, but Henry decreed that his life end with one blow of the axe. So the unconquered Thomas More climbed a shaky scaffold on July 6, 1535, and had his head lopped off. His head was stuck on a pole on London bridge for one month afterward, a trophy to barbarity. More died a martyr to the indissolubility of marriage.

Saint John Fisher was an academic who held various high positions at the University of Cambridge, one of the two universities in all of England, eventually becoming its Chancellor for life. He was a Renaissance humanist, like Thomas More, who encouraged the study of Latin, Greek, and Hebrew. Fisher was the personal tutor of Henry VIII when Henry was a boy, and he preached the funeral homily of Henry's father, Henry VII. John Fisher lived a life of extreme personal austerity and even placed a human skull on the table during meals to remind himself of his eventual end. He had many of the same qualities as More—great learning, personal uprightness, and academic accomplishments.

But easy times don't make martyrs. When King Henry wanted to annul his marriage to Catherine of Aragon, Fisher became her most ardent supporter. He openly stated in court that he would die for the indissolubility of marriage, thus incurring the lasting wrath of his former pupil Henry. All the bishops of England, save Fisher and two others, lost their courage and acquiesced, without a fight, to Henry VIII's takeover of the Catholic Church in England. Their weakness brought to a sudden, crashing end a thousand years of Catholicism in England. The faith endured in some form, of course, but would never be the culture-forming force it had been for so many centuries. It is an embarrassment of Catholic history that almost all the bishops of England fell like dominoes, one after another, at one slight puff of the breath of King Henry VIII on their cheeks.

After various nefarious machinations, John Fisher was imprisoned in the harshest of conditions for over a year, even being deprived access to a priest. During this time, the Pope named him a cardinal, although Henry refused him the ceremonial placing of the red hat on his head. After a brief trial with the usual perjury, Cardinal John Fisher was beheaded on June 22, 1535. In order to avoid inevitable comparisons between Cardinal Fisher and John the Baptist, King Henry moved the cardinal's execution to avoid any connection to June 24th's Feast of Saint John the Baptist. Both Johns were martyrs to marriage. But there was no silver platter for John Fisher. His head was placed on a pole on London bridge for two weeks, only to be replaced by Thomas More's head. Saints John Fisher and Thomas More were beatified in 1886 along with fifty-four other English martyrs. The two were canonized together in 1935.

Saints John Fisher and Thomas More, through your intercession, give all Catholics courage to resist the pressure to conform to falsehood, to the broad way, to popular opinion. You were both thoughtful and granite-like in your resistance. Help us to be likewise when times call for such.

June 24: Birth of Saint John the Baptist
First Century
Solemnity; Liturgical Color: White or Gold
Patron Saint of converts and epileptics

A rugged forerunner cuts a path for his cousin

"Dies natalis" means "birthday" or "anniversary" in Latin. But for early Christians, "dies natalis" referred to a martyr's date of death and its subsequent commemoration in the Church's liturgy, most

JUNE

typically through the assigning of a feast day. Most saints, martyrs or otherwise, are commemorated on, or near, the date of their death, the date their body was transferred to its final resting place, or on another significant date in their lives—date of ordination, coronation as pope, consecration as nun, etc. Besides Christ Himself, only two saints' birthdays are commemorated liturgically: The Virgin Mary's on September 8, exactly nine months after the Feast of her Immaculate Conception; and Saint John the Baptist's on June 24, today's feast. Saint Mary and Saint John were both sanctified, or made holy, before they first opened their eyes to the light or ever gulped a mouthful of fresh air. A long span of years did not turn them into saints. God made them holy from the start. So we commemorate their lives from the start, from their birthdays.

Only the Gospel of Saint Luke tells us the details of John's birth. John's mother and father were Elizabeth and Zechariah. They were beyond the age for having children. But Zechariah, a priest who served in the Temple in Jerusalem, was told one night by the Archangel Gabriel that Elizabeth would give birth to a boy they must name John. Zechariah was dumbfounded. Literally, when he disbelieved this annunciation, he was rendered speechless until the child's birth. When his speech was finally restored, a torrent of praise gushed out in the canticle known as the Benedictus. It is prayed as part of the Breviary every single day at morning prayer by hundreds of thousands of priests and nuns the world over. Zechariah's prayer of praise lives on.

The celebration of the nativity of John the Baptist is perhaps *the* oldest liturgical feast day in all Christendom, much older than the Feast of Christmas itself. It was at one time celebrated with three distinct Masses—vigil, dawn, and daytime—just like Christmas still is. The beheading of John, celebrated on August 29, is of equally ancient origin. The oldest liturgical books even, incredibly, indicate that there was once a liturgical commemoration of the conception of John the Baptist celebrated nine months prior to his birth, on September 24.

Today's feast is placed three months after the Annunciation, on March 25, because that gospel scene tells us that Elizabeth, John's mother, was pregnant for six months at the time. Three more months take us to June 24. (The one-day discrepancy between

JUNE

March 25 and June 24 is an accident of counting. If December and June each had thirty-one days, there would be no discrepancy.) Three related feast days line up beautifully: March 25, the Annunciation; June 24, the birth of John the Baptist; December 25, the birth of Christ. John's birth foretells Christ's birth. Although the historical chronology may not be exact, the dates show the theological interconnection among the three feasts.

All parents are naturally curious to discover the sex of their child in utero. Some allow themselves to be told the sex. Others wait in high suspense. Elizabeth and her spouse Zechariah were told by a winged messenger of God Himself that they would have a boy. That little boy grew to be a man, a great man among men who accepted death rather than swallow his words criticizing the powerful Herod Antipas. John ran ahead of Christ, clearing the ground so that the Lord's pathway would be clear. This forerunner baptized the Christ, preached and prophesied like the Christ, fasted and prayed like the Christ, and died for the truth like the Christ. But he did not rise from the dead like the Christ. There is only one Easter. We rejoice at Saint John the Baptist's birth, because what followed merits rejoicing. We rejoice at his birth, because of the generous God who intervenes in our lives, who discovers us before we discover Him.

The Youthful St. John the Baptist
Esteban Murillo

JUNE

May the birth of Saint John the Baptist deepen our love for all unborn babies, who must be given the chance to grow, to live, and to become the great men and women God invites them to be. God respected the laws of human biology when intervening in history. May we follow His example of seeing every child, every life, as a gift.

June 26: Saint Josemaria Escriva, Priest
1902–1975
Optional Memorial; Liturgical Color: White (Saint Josemaria is not on the Church's universal calendar but is included here)
Patron Saint of diabetics

Work is our sacrifice and the earth is our altar

When today's saint was a young priest, he was a rather well-known speaker in Madrid, Spain. Besides being an excellent homilist, he also preached retreats, gave parish missions, and taught classes. A young woman heard that Father Josemaria was scheduled to give some lectures nearby and, in light of his reputation, was eager to hear him. But first she went to one of his Masses. After that, the woman had no interest in hearing him lecture; instead she wanted to discover God's will for her life. Saint Josemaria's example of intense devotion and prayerfulness in saying Mass made her rethink her entire vocation. A good priest disappears into his vocation, submerges himself in Christ, and communicates a divine, not a personal, message. He makes people think of God, not him. At Mass the priest is not himself, yet is fully himself. He performs a sacrament because he is a sacrament. The Sacrament of Holy Orders is hidden behind the aspects of a man, similar to how the Holy Eucharist is hidden behind the aspects of bread and wine.

It is the theology of the Church that every sacrament validly performed is efficacious, that it transmits sanctifying grace to the soul. But the fruitfulness of a sacrament for its recipient, either psychologically or spiritually, fluctuates. It can hinge on any number of factors, from the beauty of a Church, the quality of a homily, the sacredness of the music, or the intellectual preparation and ardor of the one receiving the sacrament. A holy, charitable, and educated priest infuses every sacrament he celebrates with a theological meaning that yields spiritual fruit that goes beyond efficaciousness.

JUNE

Saint Josemaria's writings, preaching, lectures, and talks were so rich, so chock-full of practical purpose and high meaning, that a great international family gathered around him, harvesting from his sustained example and insights an abundant banquet for their spiritual table.

Josemaria Escriva was born in a small town in rural Spain. He attended diocesan seminaries in the nearby city of Zaragoza and was ordained a priest in 1925. In 1928 he experienced a vision which spurred him to found Opus Dei, an institution that quickly spread to all the major Christian countries. Opus Dei consists primarily of married lay men and women, while some members are unmarried and consecrated celibates. A few members are priests. After two thousand years of Catholic spirituality, it might be asked what new insight warranted the foundation of a new Church institution? It is a sign of the Church's theological and spiritual fecundity that Saint Josemaria did offer a new, innovative approach to living as a disciple of Christ nineteen hundred years after Christ returned to the Father.

In a homily from 1967, Josemaria states his spirituality in clear terms: "...God is calling you to serve Him 'in and from' the ordinary, material, and secular activities of human life. He waits for us every day in the laboratory, in the operating room, in the army barracks, in the university, in the factory, in the workshop, in the fields, in the home and in the immense panorama of work. Understand this well: there is something holy, something divine hidden in the most ordinary situations, and it is up to each one of you to discover it."

In other words, there is no need for a serious lay Catholic to abandon his work and routine, his family life, or his everyday relationships to fulfill God's will. God is found in and through ordinary life. Cardinal Albino Luciani, later Pope John Paul I, perceptively noted that Saint Josemaria was not teaching a 'spirituality for lay people,' as Francis de Sales taught, but a 'lay spirituality.' It is not a question of praying the rosary while sweeping the floor, or contemplating scripture while driving. It is about "materializing" holiness by converting ordinary, well-done work into a sacrifice and prayer to God. Ordinary work, then, is not just the context, but the raw material, for lay holiness. All jobs are important. Daily life is not a distraction from God's will for us. Daily life is God's will for us. When we get to work, we get to God.

JUNE

Saint Josemaria, may your intercession help us to follow your teachings in making our daily labors divine labors. May our work, well done, mingle with Christ's work and sacrifice to form one perfect offering of praise and thanksgiving to God the Father.

June 27: Saint Cyril of Alexandria, Bishop and Doctor
376–444
Optional Memorial; Liturgical Color: White
<u>*Patron Saint of Alexandria, Egypt*</u>

He was the ultimate adversary

What appears from a modern perspective to be theological hairsplitting and intellectual contortionism was, in the fourth and fifth centuries, the stuff of intense, erudite, and sometimes violent debate. Today's saint was of that heroic age when the Church, just legalized, came bursting out of her cage like a lion. She had been locked up, roaming her cramped space, half starved and small muscled when, all of a sudden, the door was lifted and the world was hers. There followed two centuries of aggressive debate, sharp criticism, harsh reactions, rough counter reactions, and prolific letter writing until several Church Councils standardized the Church's basic theology. Saint Cyril was a key actor in this theodrama. He was educated, irascible, strong willed, politically astute, brilliant, and utterly convinced that his theology of Christ was correct. It was. What mattered in the fifth century still matters today.

Saint Cyril was the Patriarch of Alexandria, Egypt, from 412–444 A.D, when it was a major city in the late Roman Empire. The Patriarch of Constantinople as of 428 was a monk from Antioch named Nestorius. He taught that Saint Mary was the Christ-bearer but not the God-bearer. Nestorius is also associated with the related false teaching that there are two hypostatic unions in Jesus Christ, one divine and one human, a theory which locates two persons in the one body of Jesus. Various critics immediately identified the errors in Nestorius' teachings, but Cyril of Alexandria was the most tenacious in denouncing him. Cyril wrote to the Pope and demanded that the Patriarch of Constantinople either retract his false teaching or be excommunicated.

A church council was called in Ephesus in 431 to settle the matter. The forceful Cyril took total command of the Council's proceedings, and, after numerous machinations as political as they were theological, the council declared Mary the Mother of God—and Nestorius a heretic. With explicit papal support, Nestorius was removed from his see. Recriminations and counter-recriminations followed, damaging the reputations of all involved. Some regions of Syria followed Nestorius' teachings and separated from the Church over the question of Christ's natures. Certain divisions remain even until today. But the teachings of the Council of Ephesus, and the related Council of Chalcedon in 451, dogmatically defined the Church's Christology for posterity. Cyril and his followers saved the day.

The theological issue at stake was theoretical, but not merely theoretical. How could one person, Jesus of Nazareth, be both fully human and fully divine? Wouldn't the superior divine nature crowd out His human nature like light crowds out darkness? Some theologians before Cyril taught that the Logos, the Second Person of the Trinity, was a replacement for Jesus' human soul. This idea was condemned. Others, like Nestorius, claimed that behind the mask of Jesus, a Logos and a human soul lurked side by side. This created problems too. Most obviously, when Jesus said "I thirst" from the cross, was He speaking as God or man? What about when He said "Before Abraham was, I am"? Who wept over the death of Lazarus? Who raised him from the dead? Who lifted the chalice and spoke at the Last Supper? Who, precisely, was the "I" of Jesus of Nazareth? The Christ riddle needed to be solved. By the early fifth century, many had tried and failed. Saint Cyril solved this perennial riddle by teaching that the subject behind the "I" of Jesus was one, not two. Jesus was a complex God-man of two natures, united in one person, and these two natures continually exchanged their respective theological and human attributes.

Despite Cyril's theological accomplishments, the tensions inherent to understanding a God-man still perdure. There are images of a tan Jesus with sandy blond hair and radiant white teeth tossing a frisbee: California Jesus. There is stained glass of a crowned Christ on His throne, scepter in hand, robed in majesty: Christ the King. And there is the wounded, naked, forlorn Jesus, hungry for air on the cross: The Suffering Servant Jesus. The Church's theology places guardrails on the road to make sure we don't veer off into heresy. Yet much is still left to the realm of prayer, spirituality, and mystery. Saint Cyril placed those guardrails. Don't go beyond here. Be careful there. Stay on the well-trod path. One person. Two natures. Indivisible. Without confusion. Perfect in Godhead. Perfect in manhood. Truly God. Truly man. Born of the Virgin Mother of God. Every heresy conquered is not a gravestone but a brick in the huge theological cathedral of the Church. Saint Cyril laid many of the bricks in the lower courses of our theological home.

Saint Cyril of Alexandria, assist and inspire all teachers, preachers, writers, and thinkers to follow your example of rigorous analysis, of fidelity to Church councils, and of understanding tradition not as an anchor but as a dynamic force.

June 28: Saint Irenaeus, Bishop and Martyr
c. 125–c. 200
Memorial; Liturgical Color: Red
Patron Saint of apologists and catechists

The Church was explicitly Catholic from the start

The iconic opening words of Julius Caesar's *Gallic War* are "All Gaul is divided into three parts." The chieftains of these three regions of Roman Gaul (France) met yearly in the southern city of Lugdunum, known today as Lyon. These rough noblemen and their large retinues trekked to Lyon in 12 B.C. for the dedication of the Sanctuary of the Three Gauls on the slope of Lyon's hill of the Croix Rousse. The inauguration ceremony was an elaborate reinforcement of Rome's military, religious, and commercial dominance. Pagan priests performed pagan rites on pagan altars to pagan gods, asking those gods to favor the new sanctuary, the tribes present, and the city. This important sanctuary remained a focal point of Lyon's civic and religious life for centuries. And in the sand and dirt of this Sanctuary of the Three Gauls, in 177 A.D., the blood of the first Christian martyrs of Gaul was spilled. Here they were abused, tortured, and executed. Killed for their faith were about fifty Christians, including the Bishop of Lyon, Pothinus, and a slave woman named Blandine. While they were imprisoned and awaiting their fate, these future martyrs wrote a letter to the Pope and gave

JUNE

ST. IRENAEUS
June 28

"For it is not needful, to use a common proverb, that one should drink up the ocean who wishes to know that its water is salt."

it to a priest of Lyon to carry to Rome. That priest was today's saint, Irenaeus.

With the dead bishop Pothinus' mutilated remains tossed into the river, Irenaeus was chosen as his replacement. He would remain the Bishop of Lyon until his death. It was in this way that the tragic end of some raised others to prominence. As the first generation of Christians in Gaul retreated from history, the great Saint Irenaeus, the most important theologian of the late second century, emerged. Copies of Saint Irenaeus' most important works survived through the ages, likely due to their fame and importance, and are now irreplaceable texts for understanding the mind of an early Church thinker on a number of matters.

Irenaeus was from Asia Minor and a disciple of Saint Polycarp, a martyr-bishop of Smyrna, who was himself a disciple of Saint John the Evangelist. The voice of Saint Irenaeus is, then, the very last, remote echo of the age of the Apostles. Similar to those of Saint Justin Martyr, Irenaeus' writings astonish in proving just how early the Church developed a fully Catholic theology.

In keeping with other theologians of the patristic era, Irenaeus focused more on the mystery of the Incarnation, and Christ as the "New Adam," than on a theology of the Cross. He also called Mary the "New Eve" whose obedience undoes Eve's disobedience. Irenaeus' writings primarily critique Gnosticism, which held that Christianity's truths were a form of secret knowledge confined to a select few. The only true knowledge is knowledge of Christ, Irenaeus argued, and this knowledge is accessible, public, and communicated by the broader Church, not secret societies. Irenaeus fought schismatics and heretics, showing just how early the connection between correct theology and Church unity was understood. His main work is even entitled "Against Heresies."

He promoted apostolic authority as the only true guide to the correct interpretation of Scripture and, in a classic statement of theology, Irenaeus explicitly cited the Bishop of Rome as the primary example of unbroken Church authority. Like Saint Cyprian fifty years after him, Irenaeus described the Church as the mother of all Christians: "...one must cling to the Church, be brought up within her womb and feed there on the Lord's Scripture." This theology notes a beautiful paradox. While in the physical order, a child leaves his mother's womb and grows ever more apart from her as he matures, the Church's motherhood exercises an opposite pull on her children. Once she gives us new life through baptism, our bonds with Mother Church grow ever stronger and tighter as we mature. We become more dependent on her sacraments, more intimate with her life and knowledge, as we grow into adulthood. The Church becomes more our mother, not less, as we age.

On Pope Saint John Paul II's third pastoral visit to France, in October 1986, his very first stop was the Sanctuary of the Three Gauls in Lyon. Excavated and opened to the public in the mid-twentieth century, it rests largely unknown, a ruin, in a residential neighborhood. Before dignitaries and a large crowd, the Pope prostrated himself and kissed the site where the many martyrs of Lyon died so many centuries before. Saint Irenaeus may have been looking on from the stone benches that fateful day in 177 A.D. when his co-religionists were murdered. The blood of those forgotten martyrs watered the seed that later flowered into the great saint we commemorate today.

Saint Irenaeus, may your intercession strengthen our wills, enlighten our minds, and deepen our trust. Like you, we want to be loyal sons and daughters of God, and loyal, educated, and faithful members of His Church. Help us to fulfill our loftiest and our most noble goals.

June 29: Saints Peter and Paul, Apostles
First Century
Solemnity; Liturgical Color: Red
Patron Saints of the city of Rome

Like the sun, Peter and Paul rose in the East but set in the West

Jesus Christ is the head of the Church. The Pope is the head of the churches. The invisible, heavenly Church, mystically depicted by the Book of Revelation and described by Saint Paul as "our mother," is the "Jerusalem above" (Ga 4:26). This perfect, inner, Church of God has theological priority over all earthly churches, which are its shadow. The first Christian congregation, in Jerusalem, anticipated and grew into the universal Church. For a short period, the Jerusalem Church was the universal church. And from this original whole, smaller parts formed, until the one Church became present throughout the world. Unity exists, then spreads. The children do not create the parents. The many dioceses throughout the world are not stitched together into a patchwork quilt called the universal Church. Catholicism is not an international federation of dioceses or the end result of its own geographic stretch. The one Church precedes the many churches. It gives them birth. The progression is from God outward, from spirit to flesh, from ontological to historical, from Jerusalem to Rome, and from Rome to the world.

All dioceses are sisters to one another. So Manila, Philippines, is a sister diocese to that of Vilnius, Lithuania; and Lagos, Nigeria, is a sister diocese to that of La Paz, Bolivia. But the universal Church is not herself a diocese. She has no sisters, lest her oneness be compromised by having a mirror church. The universal Church is a mother, not a sister. And the Mother Church was established in Rome by Saints Peter and Paul, whose feast we celebrate today. This feast also implicitly commemorates Rome's position as head of all the churches. Rome's particular vocation is to preserve the unity of God's Church on earth. This vocation is not an accidental historical addition to the Church's original nature. Unity is intrinsic to the Church's theology, and so there must be a practical force or power, internal to the Church, to preserve her unity. God's Son, after all, has only one bride, with whom he celebrates only one heavenly banquet for only one eternal, mystical wedding.

In Matthew's Gospel, Christ states in unmistakably clear language that He will build His Church on Saint Peter (Mt 16:17–19). This was not a claim from Peter but a statement of fact from Christ. For many centuries, this text has been cited in support of both Roman primacy and papal infallibility. Yet an even more fundamental historical, not biblical, fact originally supported Roman primacy. The great Saint Irenaeus in the late second century clarifies that Rome is "the greatest and most ancient Church, founded by the two glorious Apostles, Peter and Paul." No other city could claim to be the seat of two martyred Apostles. Not Jerusalem, not Antioch, and not Alexandria. Constantinople, the "New Rome," could not claim to have been built over the bones of even one Apostle. Rome's headship over all the churches is rooted most deeply in the martyrdoms in the eternal city of Saints Peter *and* Paul, the Christian counterparts of Rome's twin pagan founders Romulus and Remus.

Rome, the two-Apostle city, continues to draw pilgrims. If a plumb line were dropped hundreds of feet from the apex of the dome of St. Peter's Basilica, it would come to rest directly over the tomb of the Apostle himself in the necropolis below the Basilica's main altar. A few miles away, under the main altar of the Basilica of St. Paul Outside the Walls, lies the mortal remains of the great Apostle to the Gentiles. The inscription naming Saint Paul on an ancient marble cover for his tomb leaves no doubt whose bones were placed there. The cover even has small holes through which pilgrims could lower ribbons to touch Saint Paul's bones and thus complete their pilgrimage to Rome with a third class relic. It is a recent phenomenon to go to Rome to see the reigning pope. Traditionally, pilgrims went specifically to pray at the tombs of Saints Peter and Paul.

Our beautiful Church is a miracle. Theologically perfect but humanly flawed. Mystical and historical. All soul and all body. The Church reflects mankind—capable of so much, yet limited by her imperfections. The Church is founded upon a perfect God and two very different, great, and imperfect men whom God chose—Peter and Paul.

Saints Peter and Paul, deepen our filial devotion to our Mother the Church, who gives us life through the sacraments and who preserves our hope of attending the eternal banquet of God in heaven. Protect our Mother from corruption to be a more perfect spouse of Christ.

June 30: First Martyrs of the Church of Rome
64
Optional Memorial; Liturgical Color: Red or White

A madman burns Christians like human torches

Wave after wave of huge British and American bombers, pregnant with ordnance, opened their bays over Dresden, Germany, on February 13 and 14, 1945. Fire joined fire until the city itself was a raging, screaming bonfire. A tornado of flames hungered for oxygen, sucked all air from the atmosphere, and suffocated to death anyone caught in its vortex. The center of Dresden melted. Only some stone walls remained erect. Human skeletons were mixed into the rubble of a skeletal city. In the old town of Dresden today, a modest memorial marks a mass grave, the location where an unknown number of civilians' scant remains were cremated shortly after the fire. It's easy to walk by without noticing it. Any number of countries have similar memorials marking the mass graves of the victims of plane crashes, sunken ships, war atrocities, or natural disasters.

Many countries also have a memorial to an unknown soldier. That unknown fighter represents all those drowned at sea, lost in the jungle canopy, eviscerated by enemy fire, or simply never recovered in the heat and sweat of battle. On civic feast days, presidents, governors, and mayors lay wreaths and flowers at the graves of the unknown. In honoring him, they honor all. A nation's official remembering—in stone, statue, speech, or ceremony—preserves the past. A nation's common memory is preserved by its government, which guards against national forgetting through official acts of national remembering.

The Church's liturgical calendar is a continual, public remembering of saints, feasts, and theology, by mankind's most ancient source and carrier of institutional memory—the Catholic Church. Today's feast day commemorating the First Martyrs of the Church of Rome did not exist prior to the liturgical reforms of the Second Vatican Council. Instead, the sanctoral calendar was crowded with various feast days to particular martyrs from this early Roman persecution. Apart from their centuries on the calendar, however, little else supported these particular martyrs' existence.

Today's feast is a liturgical expression of the wreath-laying ceremony at the Tomb of the Unknown Soldier or the flowers left at a mass grave marker. This feast commemorates those unknown and unnamed men and women who were cruelly tortured and executed in the city of Rome in 64 A.D. But instead of meeting in a park to sing a patriotic hymn and to see an official lay a wreath, we do what Christians do to remember these martyrs. We meet as the faithful in a church, in front of an altar, to participate in the sacrifice of the Mass and to remember our remote ancestors in the faith who died so that the true faith would not.

JUNE

In 64 A.D. a huge fire of suspicious origins consumed large sections of Rome. A deranged emperor named The Black (Nero) blamed Christians for the conflagration and executed large numbers of them in retribution for their supposed treachery. A vivid description of the persecution survives from a Roman historian named Tacitus, who relates that some Christians were sewn into the skins of animals to be attacked and consumed by beasts. Other Christians were slathered with wax, tied to posts, and then burned alive, human torches whose glow illuminated Nero's garden parties. Still others were crucified. This was not the barbarous hacking off of limbs and splitting of skulls later suffered by missionaries in the forests of Northern Europe. Nero's madness was highly refined evil. Today, we commemorate these Christians in the same fashion in which they would have commemorated the Lord's own death—by prayer and sacrifice. We are separated from 64 A.D. by many centuries, but we are united to 64 A.D. by our common faith. We remember because the Church remembers.

Anonymous first martyrs of Rome, your blood is still wet, and your sufferings still felt, in the same Church of Christ to which you belonged through baptism. Through your intercession, help the baptized of today be as courageous as you in all things.

The Swirling Soul

Does darkness first leak from a room,
Or light rush in to surprise the gloom?

Or do darkness and light swirl and mingle,
over, under, around and through,
gusting, circling in a mysterious brew?

Every man is a world, every soul a room,
where currents and eddies push man to virtue then vice,
an unending churn and flow, first yes then no,
throwing poor man now to then fro.

M.B.

HOLY WEEK & MOVEABLE FEASTS

"My Father...let this cup pass from me..." Mt 26:39

HOLY WEEK AND MOVEABLE FEASTS

Palm Sunday of the Passion of the Lord
c. 33 A.D.
The Sunday before Easter
Solemnity; Liturgical Color: Red

Beginning with the end we understand His greatness

One way to understand a book, or to watch a movie, is to begin at the end. To read, or watch, backwards allows every character and plot twist to be interpreted in light of their conclusions. Working backwards removes much of the drama and tension from a story, of course, but it also makes the story perfectly intelligible. No slow unwinding of the plot, no "whodunit," no surprise around the corner, and no unexpected deaths. Skipping to the end makes the entire narrative clear, with prior knowledge infusing prior meaning into the story as it unfolds.

The Gospels of Matthew, Mark, Luke, and John are essentially Passion narratives with extended introductions. There is plenty of evidence that the end of Christ's life, particularly his last seventy-two hours, were well remembered by His disciples, the events being repeated in great detail until they were ultimately written down. The Evangelists eventually supplemented these often-repeated Passion narratives with further details about Christ's life which had occurred long before Holy Week. These prior narratives are often inconsistent across the Gospels, emphasize diverse aspects of Christ's life, and omit or add details in a seemingly arbitrary manner. What are very consistent, however, are the Passion narratives. Their vivid details are, without doubt, the heart and soul of the story of Jesus Christ.

On Palm Sunday we begin with the end. We read our way backwards. It is not possible for any Christian to think of Jesus Christ divorced from how His earthly life ended. Even the earliest Christian writings were composed from a post-Resurrection perspective. The "real" Jesus of history did not have miracles placed on Him like ornaments on a Christmas tree. His miracles were not later adornments hung on His human frame to lend Him credibility. The "real" Jesus is not the simple carpenter lurking in the shadows behind the Christ of Faith created by later generations. There are scant biblical references to Jesus' occupation as a carpenter, or to

HOLY WEEK AND MOVEABLE FEASTS

His simple and humble existence in a provincial town. There is a massive amount of biblical evidence, on the contrary, that Jesus suffered, died, and rose from the dead. And this biblical evidence is buttressed by an abundance of postbiblical testimony and the universal witness of an army of Apostles, saints, and martyrs.

All of this means that the "real" Jesus is the Christ of faith! The "real" Jesus did suffer, die, and rise from the dead! The "real" Jesus is not found in the *subtext* of the Gospels—He is found in the *text* of the Gospels! And those texts are indisputably ancient. In other words, the narrative read at Mass on Palm Sunday is the oldest, truest, and most well-remembered portion of one of the most fully preserved and extraordinary documents from the ancient world—the New Testament.

Our faith is rooted in history, a miraculous history. The Passion of Jesus Christ is not a parable, analogy, or metaphor. It is not a story meant to teach us a lesson apart from its facts. It is not a morality play whose actors mean to teach a lesson. The Passion of Christ is theologically significant because it is historically true. If it were not historically true, it would have no significance beyond its power to inspire as a story. But every culture already has myths to inspire its people, or at least mythical figures whose superhuman qualities model greatness. The story of Christ is so much more. It is the true story of a God-man who was betrayed by a friend, suffered calumny from His enemies, was publicly humiliated, made to carry the instrument of His own execution, and then was left to die, naked on a rough-hewn tree. This story is not sad by analogy to another story. It is sad in and of itself. This is the story we hear every Palm Sunday. This is how a great man's life came to an end. It is also the story of how the Son of God conquered death and opened the gates of heaven to all who not only believe in Him but who belong to Him through the Catholic Church.

Lord of the Passion, You suffered calumny and humiliation, You bore the Cross and did not complain. Intercede before Your heavenly Father that we may bear whatever crosses we must with fortitude. With Your grace, Lord, we can emulate You. Without Your grace, we are no better than Godless pagans, in search of frivolous signs to lend meaning to life.

HOLY WEEK AND MOVEABLE FEASTS

Thursday of Holy Week (Holy Thursday)
c. 33 A.D.
Triduum: Liturgical Color: White

No last will and testament has been as heeded as Christ's

From the moment Christ first uttered the words at the Last Supper on Holy Thursday evening, the Church has never ceased to be faithful to them: "Do this in memory of me." These words of a man about to die, if not a dying man, were a commandment more than a request, marching orders more than a mission statement. And everyone in that upper room understood exactly what He meant. No last will and testament of any man has ever been as faithfully fulfilled as these last words of Christ. What Christ asked to be done has been done, and continues to be done, every day, in every country, throughout the world, by every single priest who stands at an altar and recites the words of consecration *in persona Christi*.

The world has never moved on from Christ and never will. He is not in the world's rear-view mirror. He is here, He is present, He is alive. And in every tight corner of the globe, from a tidy Polish village to a rambling Filipino city, from a Palestinian monastery hugging a sun-baked cliff to an Argentinian parish in a sprawling suburb, the Mass makes Him real because it is done in memory of Him. Literally every minute of every day, Mass is celebrated across the globe in a ceaseless offering to God the Father. "From the rising of the sun to its setting," in a thousand tongues, priests bend slightly over their chalices and the white linens covering their altars and carefully repeat a chain of words in a cadence known to all the faithful: "Take this, all of you, and eat of it… Take this all of you, and drink from it…This is my Body… This is my Blood." No words are more familiar. None! Not Shakespeare's, not Caesar's, not Lincoln's. The everlasting words of the cross-cultural and cross-generational Christ simply have no equal.

If we expect from the Church the sacraments, we will never be disappointed. If we receive from the Church more than the sacraments, we should rejoice. The Last Supper fulfills and completes the Jewish Passover sacrifice ordered by God of Moses and the Jews in Egypt. The Last Supper, at the same time, prefigures in an unbloody way the physical sacrifice Christ would make on the

HOLY WEEK AND MOVEABLE FEASTS

morrow on the hill of Calvary. In the Last Supper, Christ also gives priests the perennial form for the Holy Sacrifice of the Mass. The Last Supper, then, is a composite act of Jewish and Christian ritual, of Old and New Testament theology, of historical and spiritual realities all packed into one dense liturgical act which the Church presents anew at every Mass. The Mass is the Christian work of art *par excellence*. It is the public act which never stops showing. It is the magnet which pulls mankind through the doors of thousands of churches every morning, noon, and night.

We do this in memory of Him because God deserves worship as a matter of justice, not charity. We do this in memory of Him because He ordered us to do so. We do this in memory of Him because it prefigures what we will hopefully do in heaven for eternity. And we do this in memory of Him for a thousand million reasons locked in the quiet places of a thousand million hearts: For Jill to come back home. So that Robert survives the war. In thanksgiving for a good husband. So that a pain in the gut not be what it might be. In gratitude for the rain that saved the crops. At a king's crowning, a convict's death, or the bond of marriage. For the shocked just after the martyrs' mangled bodies were dragged over the red sand out of the arena. In thanksgiving because my father did not die of cancer, and in remembrance of my cousin who did. For the fireman who couldn't find his way out of the building, for the barren woman, for the anniversary of an aged couple, or for the nation on its birthday. There is no end of reasons. Month after month, year after year, century after century, until the sands of time run out, the voice of the Lord on Holy Thursday echoes over the waters and down the halls of time: "Do this in memory of me." *

Lord Jesus Christ, Your total physical gift of self on Good Friday began internally at the Last Supper. May the faithful often profit from Your priestly ministry by receiving Your body and blood consecrated on Your sacred altars by those who share in Your one priesthood.

*See "The Shape of the Liturgy" by Dom Gregory Dix for a similar reflection on the Holy Eucharist.

HOLY WEEK AND MOVEABLE FEASTS

Friday of the Passion of the Lord (Good Friday)
c. 33 A.D.
Triduum; Liturgical Color: Red

No one knew love looked like this

One of the most famous Greek sculptures in the world, a larger-than-life marble statue of a female, reigns over a monumental staircase in the Louvre. A soft, unfelt breeze ripples through the thin, flowing sheets that wrap her frame. Two expansive, articulated wings sweep elegantly back from her torso, giving the impression that she has just floated down from on high and landed softly on the prow of an invisible ship. Though now headless, the statue's sense of movement is so vivid that one can still "see" her neck craning, her jaw jutting, and her eyes looking carefully downward as she settles to ground. She moves and yet she is still. She is "Winged Victory," Nike, the Greek goddess of victory.

Victory in battle, conquest in war, and success in sport are typically celebrated with a blast of trumpets, gold medals hung around the neck, ticker tape parades, a crowning with laurels, or the placing of an elegant statue like "Winged Victory" to serenely personify triumph over one's enemies. Jesus Christ changed all that. He changed what victory looked like. Jesus climbed a different podium to win a different type of victory over man's greatest enemy. On Good Friday, the God of the Living descended into the depths of human experience to conquer death. His victory parade was the carrying of the Cross on His tender shoulders up the hill of Calvary, where His hands were nailed to a splintery timber. He was raised on high by centurions for mockery, not exaltation. He then died a slow, agonizing death as His thorax sunk lower and lower and His diaphragm sucked less and less air into His lungs. It was not fast and clean. It took three hours. No one knew it at the time, but this was the new look of love in the Christian age, this was the new victory pose. Not laurels, but thorns. Not trumpets, but screams. Not medals, but scars. On Good Friday, Christ redefined victory. The victor is not prideful or strong, but humble, meek, wrecked, injured, and dead.

Pain in the non-Christian world, whether in the past or today, has no redemptive power or reward. It is just mindless, arbitrary

HOLY WEEK AND MOVEABLE FEASTS

The Crucifixion
Luca Cambiaso

suffering. At best, it is stoicism. In the person of Jesus Christ, God does not explain human suffering. Instead, He gives it meaning. And giving meaning to something is a type of answer, although not a solution. We do not go to a funeral to solve a problem. We go simply to be present, to share the family's sorrow. Sharing is a powerful response. It is more satisfying and profound to give something meaning than to make it disappear. The answer of Jesus Christ to human suffering is to share it. His answer is empathy. He suffers, dies, and is buried. No one can point a finger at God and say, "You don't know what it's like!" He certainly does know what it's like! Jesus could have saved the world by cutting Himself shaving. But He didn't. He experienced more than was necessary, because it was more fitting that God share every single human experience except sin. God drinks the common cup of human suffering to the dregs.

Jesus did not die full of years. He died young, like many tragic heroes. Christ's death gives hope to all who are preyed upon by loneliness, depression, fear, illness, anxiety, confusion, sin, and shame. In His death, Jesus does not just tell us but shows us that all these things can be conquered when united to Him. Jesus did not leave us a book. He left us a life. And that life continues to be shared with us in word and sacrament, in the fullest possible way, in the Catholic Church. God did not die on the Cross so that artists could sculpt Him. God died for a higher reason. He died for us. In Christ, the gift and the giver, the priest and the sacrifice, merge, and the result is life. As in marriage, so also in the Trinity, self-gift merges in generative love and creates life. So we etch that powerful reminder of Christ's life-generating gift of self—the Crucifix—into our tombstones and place it high in our churches. This universal symbol of redemptive love even hangs from fine chains on our necks. *In hoc signo vinces.* Christ is our new winged Victory, not with two glorious wings spreading out in a proud gesture of triumph, but with His two thin bloody arms pinned to the Cross. He hangs there in agony, gasping for air, and heroically waits for Sunday to come.

Crucified Lord, in Your passion and death, You walked for us the hard path to new life. You exited life through the door of death and so give us hope that the end is the beginning, that loss is gain, that defeat is victory, and that death is life.

"Then Peter and the other disciple set out and went toward the tomb. The two were running together, but the other disciple outran Peter and reached the tomb first."
Jn 20: 3-4

The Disciples Peter and John running to the Sepulchre on the Morning of the Resurrection

Eugène Burnand

HOLY WEEK AND MOVEABLE FEASTS

Easter Sunday of the Resurrection of the Lord
c. 33 A.D.
The first Sunday after the first full moon that falls on, or after, March 21
Solemnity; Liturgical Color: White or Gold

Checkmate!

If you want to discover what's really going on in a story, follow the women. Curious about how the plot of a book, movie, or show is going to resolve itself? Follow the female characters, because the men...and the rest of the story...will soon catch up with them. It is a female disciple, Mary Magdalen, who takes our hand and walks us quickly onto the stage of Easter Sunday. Mary doesn't go to the tomb on Saturday, because no work can be done on the Sabbath. So early Sunday, while it is still dark, Mary walks alone to the burial garden and sees something, or, more precisely, doesn't see something, that changes world history. The dead body of Jesus is not on the slab! The stone is rolled away! The tomb is empty! Mary Magdalen is witness one, the first of billions to know that Jesus rose from the dead. Witness one then quickly runs to tell the good news to witness two and three, the Apostles Peter and John. Thus the first links in the endless chain of believers were forged, a strong, enduring chain that has wended its way through history until today.

Relegating Jesus' miracles to the bin of apocryphal but consoling stories, many moderns argue Christ's most enduring legacy is the verifiable good He did for His fellow men. Yet the Gospels don't tell us that Jesus went around doing good. They tell us He went around doing miracles. Jesus doesn't help an old woman carry a load up a hill. He doesn't dig His hand deep into His pocket and spare some change. Jesus doesn't offer words of comfort to the sick; He heals the sick. Jesus doesn't jump into the sea to save the drowning Peter; He walks on the water. Jesus didn't volunteer in a soup kitchen; He miraculously multiplied bread and fish and distributed food to the masses. And Jesus didn't save people from the danger of death; He raised them from the dead. Jesus temporarily resuscitated three people, all of whom later died, before He resurrected Himself forever. There was nothing dreamy about the Resurrection. Real people with real names in a real place saw the Resurrected Jesus with real eyes. Easter celebrates the miracle of all miracles, the greatest unexpected result of all time, the indispensable genesis event of Western Civilization.

So today we raise a toast to a fresh spring morning two thousand years ago. In a garden moist with dew, with small birds chirping and flowers' bending toward the dawning sun, in a small, darkened hollow cut into the rock, a dead man, icy cold to the touch, zapped to life. He achingly rose from His stone slab and walked slowly toward the low entrance. He rolled away a heavy stone and stepped out into a new world where death was no longer the master. The ageless, see-saw battle between life and death was resolved in favor of the more powerful. Checkmate! The mind wanders at the beauty of it all.

The story is told of the conception of twins. In their first weeks of life they stretch and groan and grow. They are happy to be alive, to be together. They squirm and jostle and explore their cramped watery world. They are curious. They see a life cord tethering them to someone greater and are overjoyed. "How great is our mother's love that she shares her life with us." Weeks turn into months in their warm amniotic bath. The twins shift and change. "What does this mean?" Twin One asks. "It means that our life in the womb is ending," Twin Two responds. "But I don't want to leave the womb! I am happy here. I want to stay here forever, close to our mother!" "But we have no choice," Twin Two responds again. "Besides, maybe...just maybe, there is life after birth." Twin One: "But how can that be? The sac will break, the cord will be severed, and we'll be cut off from our source of life. And besides, there's evidence that others were here before us, and none has ever come back to tell us that there is life after birth. No, this is the end." Twin Two begins to despair, "If life in the womb ends in death, what's its purpose? It's meaningless! Maybe...maybe we don't even have a mother...maybe we just made her up." Twin One: "But we must have a mother. How else did we get here? How else do we stay alive?"

And so the last days in the womb were filled with questioning and deep fear about the future. The moment of birth came at an hour they did not expect. The twins were emotional, wondering about the unknown, uncertain if they would ever see each other, or their mother, again. The transition was painful. They struggled. They

HOLY WEEK AND MOVEABLE FEASTS

The Resurrection

heard screams. All that they knew disappeared. And then… light! Shocking bright whiteness. Their eyelids slowly peeled from their skin, and they gazed in confused wonder at a new world around them. Their life-source, their great mother, wept when they were placed in her arms. They could feel her love radiating into them. The twins were in an unknown world that calmed every fear, that exceeded their wildest dreams. Their eyes had not seen and their ears had not heard anything like this before. Their end was just their beginning. They were overcome and could do only one thing—cry out for joy.

HOLY WEEK AND MOVEABLE FEASTS

Risen Lord, strengthen our faith so that we overcome all doubt, and place our trust in Your gift of life beyond the grave. May Your resurrection from the dead inflame in us an ardent desire to be holy in this life so that we can live with You, Mary, and all the saints in the next.

Second Sunday of Easter (Divine Mercy Sunday)

Solemnity; Liturgical Color: White

True power pardons

In the Nicene Creed, we say that Jesus is *seated* at the right hand of the Father. When a judge walks into a courtroom, the bailiff announces, "All rise," and the judge sits in judgment. In his see city, a bishop rests in his *cathedra*, and in his palace, a king reigns from his throne. A president signs legislation while seated at his desk. The chair is a locus of power. The power that emanates from such seats of authority judges, condemns, and sentences. Today's feast reminds us, though, that authority also exercises power by granting mercy. When a judge pronounces innocence, the sentence is no less binding than one of guilt. The absolved exits the court into a new day, ready to begin again. And when the priest's voice whispers through the screen, "I absolve you from your sins in the name of the Father, the Son, and the Holy Spirit," guilt evaporates into thin air. The purest and truest expression of power is the granting of mercy.

Mercy is a superabundance of justice, not an exception to it. When faced with a wound to the common good, those responsible for repairing the damage do not have two contrary options: justice or mercy. Justice and mercy are not mutually exclusive. Mercy is a form of justice. Mercy does not ignore the tears to the fabric of the common good slashed by crime and sin. Rightful authority notes the torn fabric, weighs the personal responsibility of the accused, and distributes justice precisely by granting mercy. Mercy does not turn a blind eye to justice, but fulfills its obligations to justice by going beyond them. After all, one cannot be absolved of having done nothing. Similarly, where there is no guilt there is no need of mercy. When justice calls out, two words echo back off the hard walls: "condemnation" and "mercy." Mercy runs parallel to, and beyond, the path of condemnation. This is the mercy we celebrate today, the mercy whose greatest practitioner is God Himself. Because He is the seat of all authority, God is also the seat of all mercy.

God plays many roles in the life of the Christian—Creator, Savior, Sanctifier, and Judge. Our Creed teaches us that God the Son, seated at the Father's right hand, "will come in glory to judge the living and the dead," both at the particular and at the final judgment. At that moment, it will serve us nothing to state, in excusing our sins, that "God understands." Of course God understands. To state "God understands" is just another way to say that God is omniscient and all powerful. "God understands" implies that because God knows the powerful temptations of the world, the flesh, and the devil, that He could not possibly judge man harshly. Yet "God understands" is a lazy manner of exculpating sinful behavior. When nose to nose with God one second after death, the repentant Christian should plead, instead, "Lord, have mercy." Faced with the scandalous behavior of a friend or relative, the response should again be "Lord, have mercy." Appealing to God's mercy will melt His heart. Appealing to His knowledge will not.

The private revelations of Jesus Christ to Saint Faustina Kowalska, a Polish nun and intense mystic who died in 1938, are the source of the profound spirituality of today's feast. Sister Faustina was a kind of Saint Catherine of Siena of the twentieth century. She lived a regimen of fasting, meditation, liturgical prayer, and close community life that would have crushed a less resilient soul. But Faustina persevered, amidst debilitating illnesses, sisterly jealousy, and respectful but questioning superiors. Her diaries are replete with the starkest of language from the mouth of Christ, showing that moral clarity precedes the call for mercy. Sister Faustina faithfully recorded Christ's manly commands in her diary. One of these commands expressly desired that the Divine Mercy be celebrated on the Sunday after Easter. In an age-old pattern familiar to an ancient Church, Saint Faustina's private revelations were challenged, filtered for theological truth, sifted for spiritual depth, and granted universal approbation by the only Christian religion which even claims to grant such. In the soundest proof of their authenticity, the profound simplicity of the Divine Mercy revelations and of their related devotions were intuitively grasped and adopted by the Catholic faithful the world over.

Pope Saint John Paul II first inserted today's feast into the Roman calendar on April 30, 2000, the canonization day of Saint Faustina. Saint Pope John Paul II was also canonized on Divine Mercy Sunday in 2014. And so the Church's third millennium was launched with a new devotion that quickly eclipsed many older ones, a new piety rooted in the most ancient truths, a fresh appeal to a side of God that had not been fully understood in prior ages. Divine Mercy is the new face of God for the third millennium, a postmodern Sacred Heart. This is the God who leans in and waits with bated breath for us to whisper through the screen, "Forgive me, Father, for I have sinned." This is the God who at the end of time, whether our own time or all time, waits to hear from our lips those few prized words "Lord, have mercy." Having heard that, He need not hear anything more. And having received that, we need not receive anything more.

Divine Mercy, do not hold our sins against us. Be a merciful Father who judges us in the fullness of Your power, punishing when needed, but granting mercy when we need it more, most especially when we are too saturated with pride to request it.

HOLY WEEK AND MOVEABLE FEASTS

The Ascension of the Lord
c. 33 A.D.
Depending on ecclesiastical jurisdiction, the Thursday which falls forty days after Easter, or the Seventh Sunday of Easter
<u>Solemnity; Liturgical Color: White</u>

Ecce Homo...in all His glory

The heart-piercing flash of a second when the wife's eyes lock with her husband's as she steps into the lifeboat, but he stays on board the listing ship. The wailing and crying as mothers and children are ripped apart on the platform at Auschwitz-Birkenau. The well-loved cousin who leaves his far-flung relatives' home after a visit, everyone knowing he will never pass that way again. The emotional farewell. The final, bittersweet call. The last hug and tender kiss on the teary cheek. History, literature, and everyday reality are thick with dramatic goodbyes.

Departures can be painful, none more than the mysterious finality of a soul's departure from this life. For those without faith, confusion deepens the pain. Without God there is, after life, just the void. The real absence. Emptiness, chaos, and guesswork about what frightening reality awaits behind the curtain. Today's Feast of the Ascension is a peek behind that curtain and what the believer sees is life, fulfillment, and hope. In the Ascension, we have a preview of coming attractions and much, much more. Forty days after His Resurrection from the dead, the disciples witness the Lord go away. But they are not sad. Saint Luke relates that the disciples were full of joy upon returning to Jerusalem after witnessing Jesus' Ascension on the Mount of Olives. Jesus had gone away but had not died. He had departed but was fully alive. Christ showed that there was an alternative path, a different way to "do" leaving time and space.

Most memory is happy memory. We naturally forget what causes us pain and embarrassment and more easily retain what brings smiles and light. Our Catholic religion serves us well when it remembers truths on our behalf. The Church tells us year in and year out where we came from—God. It reads to us at Mass the stories of our salvation. It reminds us that death and suffering are painful but not the end. And in the Ascension the Church preserves the very positive memory of man's greatness. The Ascension reinforces our dignity. It is a shot of vitamin B right into the spine. We stand taller and straighter when we know that we are meant to live forever in the Father's house in heaven.

Many modern biologists point to a pile of wet clay and say, "Look, here is man." Modern visual artists often show bloody, suffering, degraded man and say, "Look, here is man." Sensualists sell the unclothed body to the lustful and say, "Look, here is man." Pontius Pilate stood the broken and bloody body of Jesus before the rabble and said the same, "Ecce Homo." Today the Church asks its believers to gaze up at the Ascension and to say, "Here is man too. Here is the body restored, in all of man's resplendent power." It is not enough for us to guess about our origins. We must reflect upon our destination. Where we are going says more about us than where we came from. Man is not a small pile of dirt. He is not his broken jaw, his foreclosed home, his failed marriage, or his carnal desires. He is these things, but he is more. Man is great because God is great. At Mass the priest says, "Lift up your hearts," and the people respond, "We lift them up to the Lord." Indeed. Today we marvel at the spectacle of the God-Man Jesus Christ ascending to heaven and to home. From that high place, and only from there, can we properly gauge our dignity. The Ascension should not invite speculation about the number of rooms in the Father's mansion, or how exactly the Lord zoomed up into the clouds. The Ascension is about what comes next. It's about our dignity. It teaches us that self importance is nothing. It is union with God that makes us great and makes us happy.

Lord Jesus, You were from Mary biologically but from the Father theologically. On this Feast of the Ascension, You return to the Father's house. Help all who believe in You and who belong to You in the Church to one day join You in that heavenly home forever and ever.

Pentecost Sunday
c. 33 A.D.
Sunday after the Seventh Sunday of Easter
Solemnity; Liturgical Color: Red

Happy Birthday, Church!

All living things have a birthday. The Church is a living organism and Pentecost is her birthday. Pentecost was a Jewish Feast Day. The author of the Acts of the Apostles identifies the day before the Holy Spirit ever descended. But Semitic Pentecost immediately acquired a new and perennial Christian meaning when the wind swirled and wisps of flame descended upon the heads of the Apostles in the upper room in Jerusalem. In a frightening display of God's raw and awesome power, the Lord and Giver of Life, as the Nicene Creed defines the Holy Spirit, vivified the nascent Church with fire. The Church is still vivified by that same Spirit which has never left the room. Every living thing has an *esprit de corps*: there is team spirit, company culture, a platoon's bravado, an orchestra's *élan*, or the country spirit known as patriotism. As a living thing, the Catholic Church has a Spirit too, one which indwells in her more fully than in any other Church. The Holy Spirit stamps Catholicism with a trademark of authenticity. It guarantees the Church's fidelity to the God who gave her life.

The dramatic events of the first Christian Pentecost have linked, not illogically, the Holy Spirit with spontaneity, impetuosity, miracle working, supernatural gifts, and high octane evangelization. When a throng of Christians thunders praise and makes the ground tremble, no one attributes the heaving to God the Father. When a tumor disappears and a first-class sinner publicly weeps in repentance, or when upraised hands wave to and fro, heads jut toward the sky above, bodies sway, and pores drip sweat in the heat of the night, all agree that the Holy Spirit is pulsating in sync with the mighty deeds of God. And yet…there is also the still, small voice of the Prophet Elijah. There is also the Monday morning and the Thursday afternoon. Not every day is a rollicking God party. Few days, in fact, involve rollicking God parties. Everyday life is not a crashing wave. It's more like a constant tide, rising and receding at regular intervals. The Church is often as mundane as everyday life because she is part

Pentecost
Gustave Doré

and parcel of everyday life, as a real religion should be. And so the Church's Holy Spirit is vitally present in the tide of everydayness just as she is present in the racket of a Saturday night bash.

The Holy Spirit is a spirit of unity, drawing all people toward the flame of truth. The Holy Spirit is not an alternate third column creating 'churches of one' who speak only for themselves. Christ truly desires that His followers be one, "as we are one" (Jn 17:11). The Church's unity is forged out of human diversity through a visible structure which channels the Holy Spirit through the Sacraments and their sanctifying graces. Structure and Spirit indwell. The Church's visible nature embodies the Holy Spirit in the same fashion that an Independence Day parade with its well-known leaders and predictable route embodies a country's patriotism. The tightly choreographed pattern walked by the smartly uniformed soldier at the Tomb of the Unknown Soldier causes citizens to stand in respectful silence and their hearts to swell with pride for their nation because the ceremony makes visible what is otherwise only vaguely felt. Public rituals express communally what otherwise remains emotionally elusive and difficult for individuals to verbalize. The same applies for the role of the Holy Spirit in the Church.

Watching the incense slowly rise over the altar at a solemn Mass, whispering on our knees in the deep quiet of the confessional, lighting a candle at the Grotto of Lourdes, or walking and praying as the Corpus Christi procession moves slowly forward are tangible experiences of a living Church. It is in moments such as these that we feel intensely the presence of the Holy Spirit. If we didn't feel the Spirit in these events, we would not feel His presence at all, or we would not be sure it was not, instead, just powerful auto-suggestion at work. The Church protects us from such illusions.

At Pentecost the Holy Spirit did not descend as a communal bonfire. The one Spirit of God parted and came to rest on each of the Apostles individually. The lesson? We each receive our share of God. God is the answer to the question that is every human soul. And God comes to us through a Church, not willy nilly in sweat and song. A tongue of fire is lit in every soul at baptism. We each house an eternal flame burning deep within. That flame will never be extinguished, even at death. Our personal flame of the Spirit, lit in our soul by the Church at baptism, will never die, because the Lord and Giver of Life is eternal. He waits patiently to gather together again every spark and flame that ever parted from Him into the one great conflagration of love that is the never-ending Pentecost of heaven.

Come Holy Ghost, Creator blest, fill the soul of every guest with that fire of love searing Father to Son. Hovering over the Apostles in flames of grace, You made a new high summit, the upper room, the source of unity for the human race. Holy Spirit come.

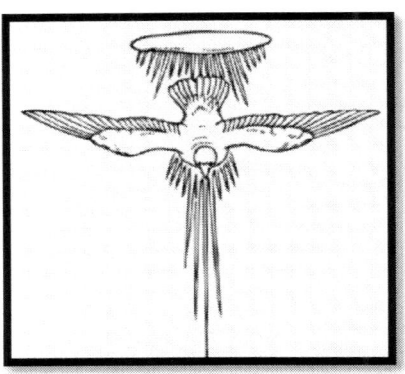

HOLY WEEK AND MOVEABLE FEASTS

Monday after Pentecost: The Blessed Virgin Mary, Mother of the Church

Memorial; Liturgical Color: White

One Mother, two motherhoods

Mary mothered Jesus, Jesus then gave life to the Church with water and blood from His side, and the Church then mothers us into existence through baptism. Devotion to Mary goes hand in hand with devotion to the Church because both are mothers. Mother Mary gives the world Christ. Mother Church gives the world Christians.

The metaphorical parallels between Mother Mary and Mother Church are spiritually rich and deeply biblical. Mary was understood by many early theologians as both the mother of the Head of the Church, Jesus, and also the symbol of the Church *par excellence*. Mother Mary is a virgin who conceived the physical body of Jesus through the power of the Holy Spirit at the Annunciation. In a parallel way, Mother Church is the Mystical Body of Christ who gives every Christian rebirth through the power of the Holy Spirit received at Pentecost. Both Mary and the Church conceived through the same Spirit, without the aid of human seed. Mother Mary makes Christ's body physically present in Palestine in the first century. Mother Church, in turn, makes Christ's body mystically present through baptism and sacramentally present in the Eucharist, in every time and place. It was common for a baptismal font in early Christianity to be described as a sacred womb in which Mother Church gave her children life.

The theological cross-pollination between Mother Mary and Mother Church has produced a field ripe for spiritual and theological cultivation. Christ is from Bethlehem, Nazareth, and Galilee. But He is most deeply from the Father. He is one Son but lives two sonships. Similarly, all Christians are born from one Mother expressed in two motherhoods: Mary's and the Church's. Mary and the Church, understood most profoundly, form one mother. Both are the mother of Christ, but each mutually assists the other to bring Christ physically, sacramentally, and mystically into the world in all His fullness. Neither Mary nor the Church can exercise their motherhoods alone.

Today's feast, formally integrated into the Church's calendar by the authority of Pope Francis in 2018, specifically commemorates Mary's motherhood of the Church rather than her motherhood of God, a feast celebrated on January 1. Mary likely showed as much tender concern for Christ's mystical body as it slowly matured in its native Palestine as she did for His physical body in Nazareth. Pope Pius XII perceptively noted Mary's dual maternity in his encyclical on the Church: "It was she who was there to tend the mystical body of Christ, born of the Savior's pierced heart, with the same motherly care that she spent on the child Jesus in the crib." It is possible the Apostles held their first Council in about 49 A.D. in Jerusalem precisely because Mary still dwelled in the holy city. She was likely the young religion's greatest living witness and pillar of unity. We can imagine her presiding over early Christian gatherings with reserved solemnity, nursing primitive Christianity just as she had Christ.

Ancient pagans spoke of imperial Rome as a *Domina*, a divine female master. Rome was praised as a conquering mother who brought vanquished peoples close to her own heart, incorporating them as citizens into her vast, multicultural, polyglot realm. Other empires executed prisoners of war, exiled peoples, imposed a foreign culture, or displaced populations. Not Rome. Rome absorbed them all. The early fathers understood Mother Church as the successor to this *Domina*. In baptism this Mother does not release her children from her body but absorbs them, making them fully her own unto death. Since the early Middle Ages, feast days and devotions to the Virgin Mary have proliferated in Catholicism. Now Pope Francis has given the Church a feast to compliment that of January 1. The two motherhoods of Mary reflect one profound truth, that Christ approaches us in time and in space, in history and in sacrament, in mysterious and beautiful ways. In the words of Saint Augustine: "What (God) has bestowed on Mary in the flesh, He has bestowed on the Church in the spirit; Mary gave birth to the One, and the Church gives birth to the many, who through the One become one." This is all cause for deep reflection.

Virgin Mary, Mother of the Church, God prepared you to be the sacred vessel to replace Mother Synagogue with Mother Church. Eve approaches you like mother to daughter, old Eve to New Eve, two mothers of the living. Help all Chritians to see both the Church and you Mary, as their mother.

First Sunday after Pentecost: The Most Holy Trinity

Solemnity; Liturgical Color: White

God is more like a family than a monk

We pray in the "name" of the Father, the Son, and the Holy Spirit, not in their "names." God must logically be only one. To hold that there is a vast government of gods is to hold that two mountains are the tallest in the world, that three oceans are the deepest, and that on four days the sun shone the brightest. Another way to say "God" is to say "the best." God is the best. And there can only be one "best," "tallest," "deepest," and "brightest." God is the ultimate superlative adjective whose nature admits of no competing god. Christian monotheism stops us from approaching different gods for different things. We believe in one God with one will, one mind, and one plan for mankind.

The Holy Trinity, the God of Christianity, is complex. Clear language must be used and clear thinking deployed to grasp the Christian God. There are no backyard garden statues of the Holy Trinity like there are of Saint Francis of Assisi, because the Trinity is cerebral in a way that Saint Francis is not. On this solemnity, we celebrate the dogma of all dogmas because dogma matters. We sing songs to dogma, put flowers on the altar to dogma, and wear our best clothes for dogma. The Church's thinking about God is not child's play. Once we accept thoughts, they own us. At some point we no longer choose our thoughts, they choose us. So we must get God right so that we get everything else right—marriage, family, work, love, war, money, philosophy, humor, religion, fun, sports, etc. Bad people can be forgiven, but bad ideas less so. And bad ideas about God are dangerous. They caused skyscrapers to crumble to the ground.

The Holy Trinity
Artus Wolffort

The Church believes that God is one in His nature and three in His persons. This means that if you were in a pitch-black room and sensed a presence nearby, your first question would be "What is that?" "Is it the dog or the cat, my spouse, or the wind?" If it were God in the darkness, He would answer the question of "what" by saying "I am God." Satisfied that the presence was a person and not an animal or the wind, the next question would be "Who are you?" And to that question, God would reply in three successive voices: "I am the Father. I am the Son. I am the Holy Spirit." A nature is the source of operations, but a person does them. A statue has eyes but it is not its nature to see. It is not man's nature to lay eggs or to breathe under water, but it is the nature of a bird or of a fish to do so. Our nature sets the parameters for what actions are possible for us. The daughter of a lion is a lioness and does what lions do. The son of a man is a man and does what men do. And the Son of God is God and knows, loves, and acts as God does, perfectly.

Our Trinitarian supernova is both a unity and a plurality, both one and many at the same time. This means that God does not exist alone but in a community of love. God is not narcissistic, admiring his own beauty and perfection. Instead, the love of the Father is directed toward the Son for all eternity. And the love of the Holy Spirit animates, and passes between, the Father and the Son. The Trinity's three persons do not share portions of the divine nature, they each possess it totally. This theology means, by extension, that because man is made in the image and likeness of God, every person is created in order to model the Trinity by living with, and for, another, just as God does in His inner life. Because God is a Trinity of persons, His perfection is more fully embodied by an earthly community, such as a family, rather than by a lone monk.

The Trinity is not just scaffolding which obscures the true face of God. Nor are the Father, the Son, and the Holy Spirit three masks which conceal the one face of God. The one God exists *as* a Trinity. The Church's belief in God and the Church's belief in the Trinity stand and fall together. The Trinity is not just the summit of our faith, something we work toward understanding, but also our faith's foundation. The truth of the Holy Trinity is learned early and often. Our God, distinct in His persons, one in His essence, and equal in His majesty, is solemnly invoked as the water spills on our heads at Baptism and as the oil is traced on our palms at our anointing. God, in all of His complexity and in all of His simplicity, is with us always in this world and, hopefully, in the world to come.

Most Holy Trinity, we look to Your three persons as a model of true love, knowledge, and community life. Help all marriages and families strive for the high ideal of perfection You set before the world, no matter the discouragement resulting from our sins and imperfections.

HOLY WEEK AND MOVEABLE FEASTS

The Most Holy Body and Blood of Christ (Corpus Christi)
Thursday after Holy Trinity unless otherwise indicated.
In the U.S, the solemnity is transferred to the Sunday after the Holy Trinity
<u>Solemnity; Liturgical Color: White</u>

The gift of all gifts

Standing at the crowded table in the dim candle light of the Upper Room during the Last Supper, Jesus Christ did not hand out Bibles to the Twelve Apostles and solemnly tell them, "Take this, all of you, and read it. This is my book, written for you." Jesus gives us Himself, not a book. On today's Feast, we commemorate God's greatest gift to mankind, the person of Jesus Christ. God gives us His Son, and then Christ gives us Himself, body and blood, soul and divinity, under the accidents of bread and wine in the Holy Eucharist. Gift, gift-giver, and receiver meld into one in this sacrament of sacraments.

In the era of the early Church, it was customary for an excess of bread to be consecrated at Mass so that the Eucharist could be carried to the sick who had been unable to attend the Holy Sacrifice. This practice led to the adoption of the pyx as the first sacred vessel for reservation of the Eucharist. Some modern churches pay homage to these Eucharistic origins by hanging an oversized pyx on their wall to use as a tabernacle, imitating the early Church custom. Permanent reservation of the Eucharist led, over the centuries, to enthroning the Lord amidst the greatest splendor in churches. By the early medieval period, the time had long passed when the Eucharist was reserved merely to be brought to the sick. Adoration of the Blessed Sacrament, street processions, chants, confraternities, songs, flowers, and all the splendid trappings of a feast day covered this dogma in glory by the High Middle Ages, and continue to wrap it in honor today.

Saint Thomas Aquinas taught that the most necessary sacrament was Baptism but that the most excellent was the Holy Eucharist. This most excellent sacrament has been, for some, too excellent. In the Gospel of John, when Jesus tells His disciples that they must eat His body and drink His blood, many are incredulous and walk away. But Jesus does not compromise or say He was misunderstood. He lets them keep on walking. This initially hard teaching for the few was destined, over time, to be lovingly welcomed by the many.

The Old Covenant of the Old Testament was gory. In a kind of primitive liturgy, Moses had goats and sheep slaughtered on an altar and their blood gathered into buckets. He then splashed this blood over the people, sealing their acceptance of the written law. Flying droplets of animal blood splattered against people's skin to remind them of their promise to God. No such bloody drama breaks out at Sunday Mass. We each bless our head and torso with holy water and receive a pure white host on the tongue. The New Covenant is based not on the blood of goats, bull calves, or on the ashes of a heifer. It is rooted in the generosity of the Son of God, who "offered himself as the perfect sacrifice to God through the eternal Spirit." Christ's Covenant with his people is established verbally and liturgically at the Last Supper and physically on the cross the following day. The consecration of the Sacred Species at Mass continues Christ's physical presence among us, while adoration of the Blessed Sacrament suspends the consecration of the Mass, stretching it out into hours, days, months, and years.

We naturally desire to leave a part of ourselves to our loved ones. We send photos, solemnly pass on a cherished memento, or give a baby a family name. Soldiers used to carry a locket holding a few strands of their wife's or girlfriend's hair. We need to be close, physically close, to those we love in concrete, tangible ways. Jesus desired the same, and, not being constrained by the limitations of human nature, He did the same, and more. He *has* left us Himself! That dogma processing down the street is a person! And that dogma behind the golden doors of the parish's tabernacle is the same person! So bend that body low and set that heart on fire, for the Saving Victim opens wide the gate of heaven to all below. We stand as close to Christ in the Holy Eucharist as the Apostles ever did on Mount Tabor.

Lord of the Eucharist, we venerate You with heads bowed, as the old form of worship gives way to the new. With faith providing for what fails the senses, we honor the Begetter and the Begotten, loving back at what loved us first, apprentices in the school of love.

HOLY WEEK AND MOVEABLE FEASTS

Sacred Heart of Jesus
Friday following the Second Sunday after Pentecost
Solemnity; Liturgical Color: White

Behold the heart which drips red for love of man

It's always the tissue of male heart muscle when the molecular structure of a Eucharistic miracle is examined under a microscope. Jesus had "heart" but, more importantly, He had *a* heart. The word "heart" is synonymous with grit, soul, intuition, love, strength, generosity, and, in its most total sense, the very center of man. Today's feast embraces all of those meanings. Christ's Sacred Heart teaches us that God loves us as a friend loves a friend, as a parent loves a child, or as a sibling loves his closest brother or sister. That is, Christ loves us *in the same way* as a person loves us, only more intensely. Our God doesn't shift the planetary order, redirect the rays of the sun, or create a parallel gravitational field to magnetize His love for mankind. Science fiction requires a fluid imagination. Understanding God's love should not, and does not, demand such mental contortionism. Understanding God's love should be as simple as recalling your little hand in your father's big hand as you walked next to him at night as a little girl. It requires remembering running into your mother's soft embrace, cheek to cheek, after skinning your knee. Jesus Christ's love for man is as human and as clear as a beating heart. Simply put, Jesus loves us from just above His solar plexus, where His heart pulsates with emotion for every sacred creature who harbors a human soul.

The widely loved devotion to the Sacred Heart is not rooted in a feast of ancient pedigree similar to those of Holy Week. No Christian of the first millenium ever gazed into the haunting eyes of Christ as He stared out from a Sacred Heart image enthroned on the family-room wall. It was only in 1856 that Pope Pius IX placed this feast on the Church's universal calendar. The Pope acted after almost two centuries of devotion to the Sacred Heart, which had grown out of the thinking, preaching, and prayer of the indefatigable Saint John Eudes and out of the visions of Saint Margaret Mary Alacoque. Both of these saints were indebted, in turn, to the medieval revelations of the Sacred Heart granted to Saint Gertrude the Great.

HOLY WEEK AND MOVEABLE FEASTS

We love the Heart of Christ because His heart loved us first. We adore the adorer, love the lover, and worship the worshiper. Because God comes first, all of our love for Him is the repayment of a debt. We are not doing God a favor by loving him any more than a hammer does a carpenter a favor by slamming nails into wood. Religion is about raw justice, not doing God favors. That God loves us is not readily apparent from creation itself or from the history of mankind. The gods were many things to many races throughout the ages, but love was not one of them. Christianity had to tell the world that God was love. And Jesus had to attach His arms to a cross and die for that message to be convincing. The visions of Saint Margaret Mary made God's love concrete and comprehensible, while the visions of Saint Faustina Kowolska deepened the meaning of this feast still more. In these challenging visions, Christ rips open His heart to Sister Faustina and shows her a calm and deep ocean of mercy waiting to bathe repentant sinners in its saving waters. Three strands—the Sacred Heart, love, and mercy—are now braided in a tight belt of spiritual truth.

True heart is not proven by waving to the crowds from a car in a victory parade or by luxuriating on the beach with friends. Real heart is in the last stretch of the neck over the finish line, in climbing the stage to receive a diploma after years of academic struggle, or in pulling yourself out of bed to go to nocturnal adoration. True heart is synonymous with long suffering, perseverance, and conquering through adversity. True heart is dying on the cross when you didn't deserve it. A true heart is a Sacred Heart. That's the heart of our God. No athlete goes to the Olympics to compete for the silver. Jesus reached for the gold from the dais of the cross, slick with his own blood. There's no need for us to keep on searching for a heart of gold in this world. We know in exactly whose body that heart beats. It's all gold, it's all sacredness, and it loves us like Himself.

Sacred Heart of Jesus, You told us to ask and we shall receive, to seek and we shall find, to knock and the door shall be opened. Today, we ask, we seek, and we knock, in the sure and certain hope that you will hear us and answer us.

HOLY WEEK AND MOVEABLE FEASTS

Immaculate Heart of Mary
Saturday following the Second Sunday after Pentecost
Memorial; Liturgical Color: White

Wing to wing, oar to oar, heart to heart

The images by which the Church describes Herself are primarily feminine—Bride, Mother, Virgin, Spouse—while masculine terms are used for the Church's ministry— the Office of Saint Peter, Office of Bishop, Holy Orders, etc. The fatherly labor and paternal structure of the Church are an outgrowth of her essentially maternal nature. *Ecclesia Mater*, Mother Church, loves with a huge heart, while Apostles, bishops, priests, and deacons hold souls together in their common mother's embrace. In the thinking of Pope Saint John Paul II, the "Marian Church," the Church of discipleship, precedes and makes possible the "Petrine Church," the Church of office and authority. So authority serves discipleship, and discipleship has preeminence over, and makes sense of, authority. Even the fatherly and authoritative Saint Paul speaks with maternal concern, calling new Christians his "children," saying he is like a "nurse" to them, and bragging that he has "begotten" them through the Gospel.

On today's Feast of Mary's Immaculate Heart, the maternal warmth radiating from the core of Mary bakes the faithful soul. Our hearts glow when we look upon the seven-pierced heart of the mother of Jesus and commiserate with the holy longing in her tender eyes. Our love for Mary also softens our love for our mother the Church. Our minds know that the Church loves us and nourishes us with sanctifying grace. But intellectual convictions need to be felt. In the same way that Christ concretely and historically images the Father, so too Mary images, concretely and historically, the Church. Mary is not a mere symbol of the Church but anticipates and embodies what she gave birth to. Absent Mary, the Church would be just a little bit too hard, too distant, and too austere. It would be like a camping site or a large, cold, house, providing shelter but lacking a woman's touch. Mary converts the dry household of faith into a cozy family home. Without her heartfelt love, the house would simply not be the same.

The prophecy of Simeon in the second chapter of Luke's Gospel is the first biblical indication of Mary's interior suffering. Simeon tells

HOLY WEEK AND MOVEABLE FEASTS

Mary that Jesus will be a sign that will be contradicted and that a sword shall pierce her own heart. Years later, Mary and Joseph panic when Jesus stays behind in Jerusalem while they return to Nazareth. When they recover him in the temple and return home, Luke tells us that Mary "treasured all these things in her heart" (Lk 2:51). At the foot of the cross, Mary's pondering heart is crushed and bewildered when sin closes in on her Son. But just when Christ's life appears to be stillborn, Mary's heart is vivified by the resurrection, and she becomes the first-century Church's indispensable witness and most sturdy anchor.

The Immaculate Heart of Mary is not a closed garden. We don't peek in through the window of the family home in Nazareth to spy Mary standing in the kitchen. Mary's life was not as public as her Son's, but it was not as private as her contemporaries. And in the Book of Revelation, her mystical significance is exposed for all to see. She straddles heaven and earth in a duel with the devil. Mary's wounded maternal heart beats strong and fast for the faithful and for the world, then, on a cosmic stage. Her heart is sinless but bruised, slit by seven swords of sorrow and dripping red for love of man. Vatican II's description of Mary as the Temple of the Holy Spirit (Lumen Gentium 52-53) implies that her heart is the red-hot tabernacle of that Temple. Today's feast was first referred to as Mary's "Admirable Heart" or "Most Pure Heart." Yet all the titles reflect the same truth; just like the love of Jesus's Sacred Heart, Mary's love for Christ and us is a tangible, human love. The Queen and King of Hearts are united in their love of all that is worth loving.

Immaculate Heart of Mary, your bruised but beating heart softens our love for you and the Church. Your love is maternal, warm, docile, and concerned. Infuse our hearts with love like yours so we can live like you in this world and the next.

HOLY WEEK AND MOVEABLE FEASTS

The Virgin in Prayer
Sassoferrato

Printed in Great Britain
by Amazon